FEMALE GENITAL MUTILATIONS

FEMALE GENITAL MUTILATIONS

THE STORY OF KEDRA

GETU TADESSE MINDAYE DR

To order additional copies of this book, contact:
Xlibris
UK TFN: 0800 0148620 (Toll Free inside the UK)
UK Local: 02036 956328 (+44 20 3695 6328 from outside the UK)
www.Xlibrispublishing.co.uk
Orders@Xlibrispublishing.co.uk
811193

CONTENTS

INTRODUCTION

Weizero Ayda Adem was born in the Shinile Farmers Association District in the Somalia region of Ethiopia (Weizero—W/o is the Amharic equivalent for Mrs.). Aida is hot-tempered, straightforward, and generous. She has tremendous respect for her tribal culture and Muslim religion.

Being a conservative Muslim, Ayda is committed to the laws and orders of the Holy Koran. Although she is aware of the merits concerning education, W/o Ayda does not accept the importance of education for herself. She does not want to become an outcast from her tribal traditions. Despite this, W/o Ayda tries her level best to send her son and daughters to school. She sees other families enjoying a better life by reason of their education and wants the same for her children. In this regard, she is more progressive than her husband, Ato Hajji Hussein (Ato is the Amharic equivalent for Mr.).

In contrast, Ato Hajji wants his children and his family to be good Sunni Muslims. He believes that only males are family leaders, in accordance to the tradition of his clan. Males need to go to school, and females should respect the family by raising children and being homemakers. Ato Hajji despises girls' education. For this reason, their first daughter, Amina, at age thirteen, was taken out of the seventh grade to marry. She birthed two children after marriage. However, her youngest brother, Ali, is twelve years old and will continue his education. W/o Ayda's youngest daughter's name is Kedra, she will attend Koran school during her early years and will only experience secular school until she is proposed to in marriage. The other two children, Nadia and Farah Hussein, from Ato Hajji's second wife, attend Koran school before they are permitted to attend secular education.

Ayda married Ato Hajji Hussein when she was seventeen old. Hajji is the Islamic honorific title for the person who has completed the pilgrimage to Hajji. It is a title given to a respected elder. Mecca is the holy city of Islam in Saudi Arabia. Ayda dreams of raising her children in a better school district and wants to move her family to the modern city of Dire Dawa.

Though Amina used to dream of attaining a higher education, her ambitions were handicapped by the family's enforcement of marriage at a young age. Amina is quite sad and upset about not being permitted to achieve her goals. She blames her stubborn family for her loss. Nowadays, Amina lives with her husband in the city of Dire Dawa in a village called Hafetesa.

I invite you to sit back, grab a box of Kleenex, and experience a woman's heartfelt journey. This woman was born in Ethiopia, and her life was written and orchestrated by her family's traditions, cultures, and religion. *This book* is sure to move you in unimaginable ways. Although the introduction introduces a strong Ethiopian family, this book focuses on the heartache of the youngest child born into W/o Ayda's family: Kedra.

CHAPTER 1

THE EARLY YEARS

Six-year-old Kedra lives in Shanelle, a small neighborhood in the Somali region of Ethiopia. She spends her leisure time interacting with her peers, running, playing hopscotch and hide-and-seek, and making dolls out of mud. Kedra is the youngest daughter of the three children born to Weizero (W/o) Ayda and Ato Hajji Hussein. She is loved. The parents tend to spoil her with gifts such as clothing, dolls, and of course, her favorite traditional sweet treat, baklava. The children feel special and important when they receive gifts because it rarely occurs in their culture due to most families not being able to afford frequent purchases like in the United States. Baklava is a scrumptious pastry that is made of halwa (wheat flour), melewa, sugar, oil, and butter. This flaky, delicious treat originated in Turkey, but it was adopted into the East African culture.

Kedra, as with all girls her age, wakes up at daybreak to veil her hair, pin her ears, and eat breakfast before attending Koran school. Pinning your hair represents Muslim dogma. Kedra is unsuspecting and naive to the cultural and religious rituals of her parents. Kedra is of age to complete a traditional ceremony that has been practiced for thousands of years. It will change her life forever. Her parents have planned this ceremony to take place very soon—with or without the child's consent.

On the eve of her ceremony, Kedra's father, Ato Hajji Hussein, is conversing with W/o Ayda on the veranda, he is holding the qat leaves that will be chewed during an afternoon ceremony, while waiting for his colleague Mustafa.

* * *

Qat (called *khat* in Amharic) is a well-known drug called *Kata adulis*, which grows in Eastern Africa and Yemen. The shrub that grows in Ethiopia and Kenya is especially known for its feeling of euphoria and sedation, which block the entire sympathetic nervous system. The leaves and buds are chewed in ceremony. This practice is habit-forming because of its narcotic effects. In the past, qat was used to stay awake all night for Muslim religious rituals and for personal pleasurable use. However, since the fourteenth century, qat is mostly used as a means of passing the time, particularly in the southern Red Sea region.

In Eastern Africa and Yemen, scores of people spend their leisure time chewing qat. In Dire Dawa and other neighboring Eastern Ethiopian cities, qat is not only taken as a pastime, it is indigenous to Somali culture. An outsider might be surprised to see the widespread observance of qat—and the fact that so many women host qat ceremonies.

Every chewer seeks to get their qat at opportune times, usually from noon to three in the afternoon, when the sun is high and the air is thin. Qat is a respite from the scorching heat. The qat can be enjoyed after lunch without interruption. Some chew with regular water, and others chew with mineral water or soft drinks. Qat is never used with alcohol because it is believed that alcohol interferes with the sedation-euphoric affects.

After four or five hours have passed, Christian and affluent-class chewers often go to bars to drink alcohol. The poor consume locally made liquors. Alcohol is consumed afterward, rather than during, to remove and break the effect of the qat and the feelings of depression. On the other hand, Muslims will drink hot milk and wait out the depressed mood. The milk is believed to cool warm blood and regulate body temperature.

Usually, most qat ceremonies are staged in groups with individuals sitting on a floor mat or a mattress. Though qat ceremonies are primarily East African cultural traditions, men and women must chew separately in accordance with their long-held tradition. The chewing ceremony is celebrated with incense, music, radio, or even television shows. It is also the women's responsibility to host and serve coffee and tea during the qat-chewing ceremony.

During a qat ceremony, a range of ideas will be raised and discussed by the attendants. At the beginning of the chewing ceremony, there is usually lively discussion, gossip, and making fun. By late afternoon, moods become sedated due to the increased consumption and the effects of the drug, resulting eventually in a depressed mood. During such times, everyone concentrates on future plans with feelings of conquering the world. Physiologically, heart rates and blood pressure have increased, and there is heavy sweating. Nevertheless, every participant drinks tea or coffee and continues to chew.

There are three chewing periods in the day. In the morning, *Yejebna* is chewed to stimulate the nerves. It is only for short periods of time. This creates a type of eye-opening experience to alertly begin one's day. Next, there is what the chewers in that region call *Bercha*, where most of the community partakes in an afternoon qat chewing. Comparatively, it takes much longer and is intended as a pastime. Bercha is a citywide practice among Christians and Muslims alike. The last is called *Katira*, which takes place in the late evening. It is intended to keep participants awake and alert to discuss important issues and to perform nightfall *sigidet* (prayers). Katira extends until dawn. Normally, elders and older persons participate in Katira.

In this Eastern Ethiopian community, qat sales begin very early in the morning. The cities become crowded with citizens moving about, farmers on camels or donkeys transporting their qat for sale, and merchants transporting qat into the city. Qat commerce significantly contributes to the city's rush hour. By afternoon, the city calms to a complete silence because everyone sits and chews qat, and the drug sedates everyone and makes them passive and dormant. After Bercha, merchants may forget appointments, and sellers may forget the prices of products and services! Due to the drug-induced depression and forgetfulness, some people become stressed, anxious, or even dizzy.

* * *

W/o Ayda stares at Ato Hajji and says, "How did we get careless with this girl? Look! Kedra is growing and is already six years old."

Ato Hajji promptly replies, "We were never careless!"

W/o Ayda says, "As you very well know, she is getting older. It will be difficult to circumcise her!"

Ato Hajji, holding his ritual qat in one hand and reclining on pillows with his other hand, replies, "What are you saying? This practice is highly criticized and denounced. Even recently, religious leaders and medical experts exposed the dangers of circumcision. So how dare we let our daughter become circumcised?"

W/o Ayda is surprised by Ato Hajji's comments and stares at him. "What is wrong with you? You understand the matter more than I do. It is our religion and custom. It is disrespectful and will bring humiliation to our family if we let our daughter go uncircumcised! Who is going to marry Kedra? You know, if a girl is not circumcised, she is not considered to be a virgin or clean. For this reason, we allowed our older daughter to become circumcised. Amina has been respected for that—and so have we as her parents. Do you forget that you made sure these things were carried out before we were married?" Ayda stares at Ato Hajji.

"Of course, we respect our culture and religion—and what they preach at the mosque is true. However, do you remember the daughter of our colleague, Ato Ali Hussein? She passed away due to circumcision complications. Do you also remember that other children's lives were lost due to similar problems caused by circumcision? Even if they did not die, their suffering during circumcision was terrible! Don't you remember that our daughter, Amina, suffered a lot during circumcision? So, how dare we repeat that same pain and anguish one more time?"

W/o Ayda laughs and says, "What do you mean? You are not aware that you are prestigious and a stakeholder in the village?"

Hajji replies, "Of course, I know society gives me some sort of reputation and prestige. Nevertheless, our Holy Koran does not state even one word regarding circumcision. Though we may not be educated, sometimes we should listen to what the educated people tell us not to do."

While Ato Hajji is ritualistically praying, there is a knock at the door. W/o Ayda orders Kedra to open the fence door. After opening the door, W/o Ayda tells Kedra to enter her bedroom. The visitor is Ato Mustafa, an old friend and a neighbor of Ato Hajji. He is dressed in a striped apron tied with his belt, a white T-shirt, and leather sandals. He is ready to partake in the qat ceremony. Mustafa's henna-colored, plated mustache is reddish and is considered to look good among his peers. Ato Mustafa is four years older than his friend Ato Hajji.

They greet each other with the traditional Muslim handshake because that is the common and polite greeting. However, men shake hands only with men, and women shake hands only with women. The right hand is considered the clean and polite hand to use for eating, writing, and shaking hands. If the child shows a left-hand preference, the parents will train them to use their right hand.

W/o Ayda orders Kedra to bring pillows as a back support for the guest and invites him to sit on the already made mattress for the qat ceremony. W/o Ayda asks Kedra bring mineral water from the neighbor shop because it will be served with the qat.

The conversation about circumcision is interrupted when Ato Mustafa arrives.

Nevertheless, W/o Ayda continues her dialogue with her husband, even though she knows that circumcising the girls is her duty. Ayda says, "We've had some serious discussion, and it is nice of you to listen to us."

Ato Mustafa says, "What was your issue of discussion?"

W/o Ayda says, "We were dealing with Kedra's circumcision, but your colleague, Hajji, is arguing against it."

Ato Mustafa says, "How dare you say that she shouldn't be circumcised! What is wrong with you? This must happen!"

Ato Mustafa has eight children from his legal wife, including five girls. His first daughter, Rehima, migrated to Djibouti and grew up there. Therefore, she did not to get circumcised. However, the rest of the sisters have had the tragedy of circumcision performed in the Shinile region where they reside.

Rehima's sisters are all married, but nobody wanted to marry Rehima because she was uncircumcised. She was finally circumcised by force when she was twenty-six years old. At twenty-six, Rehima is considered to be very old for marriage. Considering this, she remains single even though she completed the painfully traumatic procedure. Instead, she ended up with a medical disorder, desperation, and frustration. As a result of Rehima's circumcision, in the past four years, she has been hospitalized several times and has had numerous operations due to complications from the procedure.

Reminded of his daughter's suffering and pain, Ato Mustafa says, "It is ridiculous and a shame to let an uncircumcised girl live in your home. This does not only let her commit intercourse, but also the community at large disrespects and will isolate you. Look! Do you really know how much trouble I am in because of my older daughter? Even though I can see my grandsons from her younger sisters, I cannot see Rehima's children. She couldn't find anyone to marry her because she was not circumcised and sewed. For this reason, she has remained single. You should keep your reputation and continue being a model for others."

W/o Ayda is delighted to hear Mustafa's comments. She says, "Those who are teaching about the dangers of our daughters' circumcision and sewing are ones who know nothing about the benefit of it. What they say is nonsense! In my view, I am afraid of being an outcast and becoming isolated if we do not have Kedra circumcised. We had better circumcise her just like her peers—and accept the pain and tribulation that comes after. We have to live in peace and harmony with the community and keep our reputation."

Ato Hajji knows that his daughter's circumcision is a wife's duty. He says, "Everything you said is true. I am not denying the facts. However, circumcision is taught against in schools, hospitals, clinics, and even the mosque. Though we are not educated, we must listen to what the intellects say. In addition, this is not the law of the Koran."

Ato Mustafa picks up a qat stick and stares at Ato Hajji. "What is wrong with you, my brother! Don't you remember that in our weddings, our brides were checked for circumcision and sewing. If this girl is not circumcised and genitals sewed, and as a result becomes pregnant, you can't imagine the humiliation you will encounter!"

Ato Hajji fails to convince them to change their minds about the undue pain and useless procedure that has been a long-held tradition. He says, "According to the law of the Koran, this is strictly forbidden." He finally concedes to his wife's wishes to remain well seen in his culture. In the final analysis, Ato Hajji fears rejection and isolation within the community in which he resides. Ato Hajji finally agrees it will be in the best interests of the family to have Kedra circumcised and sewed for the sake of keeping his family's honor.

W/o Ayda cannot know that her daughter may be circumcised—whether Ato Hajji agrees on the matter or not. She plans to circumcise Kedra while Ato Hajji is out on business or similar affairs. She is certain that she will follow through with the tradition according to their beliefs. However, she is very pleased that Ato Hajji has been persuaded.

Ayda is very happy and says, "It is nice of you to have agreed on the circumcision for Kedra. Just think of the isolation and humiliation that we could face if she was not circumcised. By being circumcised, Kedra will keep her virginity and eventually engage in legal marriage. That is triumphant even for us. Kedra will appreciate our decision as she matures and will embrace the importance of being circumcised."

* * *

According to numerous documented sources, female circumcision began in the Arab Peninsula in Egypt around the fifth century BC. Though it is difficult to be certain, female circumcision was practiced among ancient Arab traders, and they brought the practice to Ethiopia. Presently, female genital mutilation is practiced all over the country: north, south, east, and west. Girls undergoing the procedure have varying degrees of knowledge about what will happen to them both during and after the long-held traditional procedure. The tragic event, however, is associated with festivity, gifts, and sometimes new clothes to lessen the concern.

Female genital mutilation is a very dangerous bloody practice because too many girls bleed to death. Such complications can be very serious, and the recovery takes a long time. In Ethiopia, there are four types of circumcision. Type 1 (Sunna) involves removal of the skin surrounding the clitoris (clitoral prepuce) with or without excision of part or the entire clitoris. When this procedure is performed, most of the time, the clitoris and surrounding tissues are damaged. Type 2 (clitoridectomy) is a removal of the entire clitoris. Type 3 (excision) consists of the removal of the clitoris, labia majora, and labia minora. Type 4 (infibulation or paranoiac circumcision) involves the removal of the clitoris, labia majora, labia manor, and part of the vagina. The remaining tissue is sewed, leaving only one small opening where there were two: the vaginal orifice and the urethral orifice.

According to the Ethiopian Demography and Health Survey (DHS), 73 percent of females in Ethiopia are at least victims of one of the four types of circumcision. In the eastern region of Ethiopia, among Somali nationalities, 97 percent of females are exposed to the most extreme circumcision in the world: infibulations. The remaining 3 percent are either underage to be circumcised or are very lucky.

Both males and females are typically circumcised before age five. Male circumcision may be performed by traditional doctors or by a medical doctor or nurse in a hospital, health center, or clinic. Alternatively, female circumcisions are usually performed by traditional practitioners who are generally elderly women in the community who generate their income off this type of procedure; they may also be traditional birth attendants.

The reason for female circumcision is dependent upon the culture and tradition of the respective community. For instance, eastern region communities consider the clitoris to be filthy, foul smelling, dangerous to the life of the new baby, hazardous to health, and disruptive to the husband's potency. Others claim that circumcision and sewing (infibulation) helps women remain virgins and protects them from rape as well as pregnancy before marriage. Moreover, it is believed that during sexual intercourse, females' sexual desire and sensation are more pronounced than their male counterparts. By removing parts of girl's external genital organs, sexual desire is minimized, and a delicate balance is created. This makes men more apt to match and satisfy females' sexual orgasms. Theoretically, a sexually dissatisfied woman is less likely to seek satisfaction from other lovers if her own desires are diminished by mutilation.

* * *

The wind has stopped blowing, and as the sun sets, the daylight quickly gives in to the night. This is the time of the day when the weather is cooling, and more people pass through the village. Ato Hajji and Mustafa are holding qat while sipping tea and water to swallow their chew. They continue discussing religion, business, and social affairs.

Amina, Hajji and Ayda's eldest daughter, arrives from Dire Dawa and delivers the traditional greetings before entering the home. Amina finds her mother and Kedra chatting.

W/o Ayda tells her daughter that it is great to see her and expresses her gratitude for coming.

"Why the thanks?" asks Amina.

"I will tell you later," W/o Ayda replies. "First, you better have your lunch before you become tired. Then we will go somewhere."

After Amina has lunch, they go to the market to purchase commodities for the event.

Kedra is instructed to stay home. As usual, she goes out to play with her peers.

W/o Ayda tells Amina that W/o Seida will be called to come and circumcise Kedra on Sunday morning, and there will be a large celebration that Amina must attend.

Astonished by her mother's decision to circumcise Kedra, Amina screams, "Is Kedra really going to be circumcised?" She stands up and sits down again.

Ayda asks, "What is wrong with you? What makes you so surprised?"

"Why don't you stop this thing? The suffering and tribulation that happened to you and me is bad! Do you want to see that pain and misery happen to your innocent little girl once again?"

"Stop it!" Ayda says. "It is none of your business! You are too young and immature to advise your mother!" She tucks in the waist of her dress.

Amina says, "Mom, why don't you listen to me? You always think you are right since you are older. Don't negate the fact that I have been through this and have experienced the negative effects. My outlook—though not knowledge-based from school—is correct. In public meetings and on the radio, this cultural practice is discussed as having nothing but health complications and physical disorders. At least I am a bit more literate than you. I understand that this is a tradition that holds some weight within the community, but it is an outdated practice that causes us, as women, to suffer. There are plenty of girls who engage in legal marriage who have kept their virginity without circumcision. What surprises me is that women who have been victims of circumcision will allow their daughters to become victims. Please leave my innocent little sister alone. I beg you to not allow this to take place again."

"Stop it!" Ayda says. "It is none of your business! You are not the one to pass judgment about circumcision. Don't give me a lesson. You cannot dictate what we have been practicing for so long as the code of conduct in our culture and tradition. As a mother, I have the responsibility to make sure my daughters are circumcised because I believe this is important and necessary for her and for the parents. We are going to do it because we believe in it and wish to keep the tradition. Moreover, it is the sign of decency and the virginity of a girl. We have to keep our dignity in the community. Our daughter will grow up free from rape and harassment—just like you."

Amina's eyes are full of tears. "Do you think that being circumcised will save her from having sexual intercourse? Don't you remember my sufferings?"

Ayda says, "You suffered a lot, and we shared your pain. However, everything is forgotten now. Nowadays, you are okay. We have offered you to a very good husband with prestige and reputation. It is better to let Kedra become circumcised and take the risk and feel the pain than for her to suffer isolation and humiliation in our community. We better go to the market to shop for chicken and clothing for Kedra. Besides, there are other things that we have to buy for the event."

Amina says, "It is very unfortunate that women's suffering is beyond belief. Our illiteracy is attributed to all this. We are born to satisfy men's sexual desires, and we suffer tribulations and anguish throughout our lives. We are victims for such traditions. When will this be over? By the way, does Dad agree?"

W/o Ayda is irate at the continual defiance of her daughter, but her toothless half smile lights up her face. "Whether he agrees or not, it is mandatory. Let's leave!"

Amina and her mother travel to the marketplace to purchase clothes, toys, and chicken for the celebration after the circumcision. The women stop at Ato Hajji's second wife's textile shop to invite her. She was married to Ato five years ago—after she was forced to quit school during her sixth year to marry because her family was poor. The suitor offered five camels and five thousand Ethiopian birr.

W/o Kaltum bore three of his children to enrich his clan/tribal line. She is lonely, raising their children alone is and not happy in their marriage, but she acknowledges that the Holy Koran declares the supremacy of men and lives in despair. Although she considers herself to be very unfortunate because she had to drop out of school, she is quite successful. W/o Kaltum is popular in the market because she extends credit to customers; however she is successful with her crafts and home decorations. Considering her business transactions and strict religious fellowship, she is seen as a decent person. She enjoys listening to all the stories people have when they come in to her shop. W/o Kaltum thinks dropping out of school was the biggest problem in her life. She often reads books, including the Holy Koran. Because of this, W/o Kaltum gives exhaustively to her children so they will not have the same fate. She is an advocate for education and gives similar advice to anyone who is eligible for school.

Ato Hajji married W/o Kaltum to attain his ambition of delivering an enormous number of children to enrich his tribal line or clan. Ato Hajji spends most of his time with his first wife. This makes Kaltum feel lonely because she is raising three children virtually on her own. The Holy Koran declares the supremacy of men. Nevertheless, Kaltum acknowledges that she lives in despair and is very well aware of what her marriage to Ato consists of. She often discusses males' supremacy over females' illiteracy with her husband's daughter, Amina.

While Kaltum is serving clients in her store, she looks up and sees W/o Ayda and her daughter coming in to the shop. As usual, they exchange the customary Islamic greeting for women and then were invited in and offered Coca-Cola. It is a time-honored gesture of honor to offer a soda, juice, or tea—something other than water or alcohol.

Water is ordinary and can be offered anywhere by anyone, and alcohol is forbidden.

W/o Ayda invites W/o Kaltum to the ceremony and says that they came to shop for the necessary materials for the ritual.

W/o Kaltum asks, "Why do we let our children become victims of this harmful cultural stigma and suffer? Our society is conservative when it comes to culture and taboos. We should differentiate between the culture and religious law and relieve the suffering and anguishes of others. Culture is not by any means interpreted as tribulation and suffering of our children."

W/o Ayda asks angrily, "You're like that too? Your daughter is mine, but I don't insist on you changing your decision."

W/o Kaltum replies, "I was simply offering my opinion on matters that I don't accept."

W/o Ayda asserts that a girl should be circumcised to keep her virginity and dignity for the social good.

Amina, pleased with W/o Kaltum's opinion, says, "This custom is worthless for females—and for males too! The entire ritual is based on satisfying males' sexual libidos, relieving their fears about female sexuality, and boosting their egos by discarding female genital organs. There are even females who favor it. This practice should be stopped!"

W/o Ayda says, "The Almighty has not given me a daughter who commits intercourse before marriage. Those who commit this sin in front of Allah are disgusting! Anyway, you better come on Sunday morning as I told you. There are some tasks that you have to help with." Ayda exits the shop.

Amina is outraged by the ignorance of her mother, putting her own pride above the lifelong mental and physical well-being of her daughter for a customary barbaric circumcision. Amina takes a deep breath. Upset or not, she knows that she will not be able to convince her mother otherwise. Her only recourse is to finish gathering the remainder of the presents and shop for the chicken to be prepared at the circumcision ceremony.

After the qat ceremony, Ato Hajji and Mustafa are ready to go downtown to relax and refresh.

W/o Amina and her mother come home from shopping with three chickens, clothes, shoes, toys, and other things to prepare for the ceremony. W/o Ayda puts away the commodities, Amina returns to

Dire Dawa, and then Ayda goes to find the most renowned lady in circumcision: Seida Omar.

W/o Ayda discovers W/o Seida standing in her dining room and asks to enter her home after exchanging customary greetings.

Ayda says, "I would like you to circumcise our daughter whom you helped deliver five years ago."

W/o Seida smiles. "How fast time flies! I'm surprised that I am going to circumcise a girl who I helped deliver only five years ago. Time and tide wait for no one. I don't believe that she has already grown ready for circumcision. It means that we are getting older at the same pace. Oh, yes! This is my duty. I will be there in the morning to perform the procedure."

W/o Ayda says, "I, of course, know that it is your duty. I was just letting you know ahead of time."

"Don't worry," W/o Seida says. "I will be there in the early morning."

Upon hearing this confirmation, W/o Ayda returns home.

Seida charges thirty birr per circumcision, which amounts to approximately $1.50 in US currency. Seida prefers money to the suffering of innocent child victims.

It is dark when Ato Hajji gets home. He speaks with his wife about Kedra's circumcision.

W/o Ayda tells him that W/o Seida is coming the day after tomorrow to perform Kedra's circumcision.

Ato Hajji says, "Have you totally decided that she will be circumcised? I can't help it! Do it as you wish."

Ayda says, "We better not discuss this topic anymore. We have already agreed and decided. You better think about the goat that you have to buy on Saturday morning."

Ato Hajji is the dominant decision-maker in family matters, but he fails to convince his wife today. With his daughter's circumcision, he feels powerless. He is worried about the isolation and being cast out from the community if Kedra is not circumcised. If he rejects the deep-rooted ritual, he will be held in contempt in the eyes of his peers and leaders. He agrees to buy the goat and slaughter it on Saturday morning. He feels like that there is nothing else he can do on Kedra's behalf.

When Mohammed and Kedra get home, Kedra says, "Mom, you have gone shopping today? How dare you not bring mushebek for me?"

W/o Ayda looks down at her and says, "I brought you something better than mushebek. I will show it to you the day after tomorrow.

Anyway, I brought you mellewa." Mellewa is a sweet cookie that is similar to a baklava.

Kedra holds her mother's dress and kisses the hem. She dances around her mother and sings to her. She runs and shares the treats with her brother Mohammed. She is unaware of the fate that awaits her.

Ato Hajji stares sympathetically at his daughter. He is mindful of Kedra's naiveté regarding the rapidly approaching ritual.

Kedra returns and asks, "What else did you buy for me, Mom?"

Her mother says, "You will find out on Sunday morning."

Kedra says, "Why the day after tomorrow? If it is for me, why is it important to wait until then?"

Ato Hajji thinks about the suffering and anguish she will experience on Sunday morning.

Her mother says, "You will be recognized by your peers after you are circumcised. You will then accept and cherish the many gifts that will be brought to you."

Kedra has heard all about the suffering and pain of circumcision from her peers. She says, "I will never be circumcised!" She throws the mellewa on the floor.

With a sympathetic smile, knowing Kedra is powerless and can do nothing to prevent the tradition from taking place, W/o Ayda says, "If that happens, I won't give you what I bought for you." Ayda and the other mothers in the tribe understand that the decision is to be made by the mothers alone.

Kedra starts crying and yells, "I won't be circumcised! I will run away!"

W/o Ayda says, "Don't worry. You should not say that. All your peers are circumcised: Nefisa, Awa, Kaltum, and your older sister, Amina. This is not new to you, and you know all of these girls. Even I was circumcised. It was quite normal. Nothing happened to me, and nothing happened to your peers. So, you have to become just like them. If you are not circumcised, they will eventually cast you out. They will tease and laugh at you. In the future, no man will want to marry you." W/o Ayda tries to convince her daughter that this is for the best.

Kedra continues to adamantly plead and cry to her mother.

Mohammed says, "Kedra, are you crying about your circumcision? If you are not circumcised, your peers will laugh at you. They will tease you about being uncircumcised. In the future, if men are aware that you are uncircumcised, they will rape you and mock you."

Mohammed's words frustrate Kedra even more.

Ato Hajji says, "It is okay, my daughter. You will only feel the pain once. You have to show them that you are not more inferior to your friends."

Mohammed says, "Boys do not marry uncircumcised girls. Look, Ato Mustafa's daughter, Rehima, is now old but not married. Therefore, we need you to be circumcised."

Kedra feels all the sympathy and soothing from her brother but remains extremely upset. She refuses to eat dinner and eventually falls asleep on the sofa.

CHAPTER 2

STRIPPED OF INNOCENCE

Sunday, the day of Kedra's circumcision, is a bright warm morning. Kedra is visibly anxious and exhibits behaviors of someone who will soon be tortured. She is overwhelmed by thoughts of her friends, sister, and mother having been circumcised from their own accord. Kedra is strongly opposed to the process. Even though her brother tries to soothe her with convincing statements, she remains withdrawn and silent.

Her peers and stepsiblings come to celebrate the circumcision ceremony. By eight o'clock in the morning, everyone is in high spirits, eager to begin the ceremony, and dressed in their finest clothing. The children are running around, singing, playing music, and dancing. The delicious aromas of rice, vegetables, and meat fill the air. Almost every female in attendance has been a victim of circumcision. Kedra is extremely scared and doesn't want to suffer the same fate.

In just a few hours, Kedra, like her relatives, friends, and other women in the community, will have her genital organs removed and the remaining tissue sewed. When this cultural practice is complete, she will be highly regarded like her circumcised peers, and she will be able to keep her good reputation as per the long-held tradition of the community.

As the pre-festivity celebration continues and the ceremony grows both inside and outside the house, the neighborhood is sharing the workload. The women in the community are preparing succulent traditional dishes that can be smelled for a mile. The neighbors have brought candy, chewing gum, and cookies for the young girl who is going to be circumcised. She will subsequently earn a prestigious reputation per the code of conduct of the community. Some of the guests are sitting on long wooden benches, and others are standing.

W/o Ayda is preparing the chicken that Mohammed butchered, and he and his father will slaughter the second goat and chop firewood to sacrifice the chicken.

Ato Mustapha has come early to help his friend, Ato Hajji.

Amina has come from Dire Dawa with her children. She sees Kedra crying and says, "Don't worry. It is not that painful. You can handle it." She discretely enters an unoccupied room to hide her sorrowful tears.

Ato Hajji's second wife comes early and says, "W/o Seida has not yet come?"

W/o Ayda turns to her and says, "She will come right at eight o'clock. Until then, you can prepare the coffee."

W/o Seida is on time as usual. She is carrying her small aluminum-plated box that holds circumcision equipment. The customary greetings are exchanged, and she goes into the designated circumcision room to prepare for the procedure.

In the room, Kedra is paralyzed with fear.

W/o Seida tries to reassure Kedra by telling her not to be afraid.

Kedra screams and cries loudly at Seida's arrival, and she tries to escape by running out of the room. "I won't be circumcised!"

Kedra's mother shouts, "Catch her! Catch her! Follow her outside!"

Mohammed and Amina's son, Farah, run after Kedra.

She tries to resist her brother and nephew by rolling on the ground, but they overpower her and take her back where she has no chance to run again. As an extra precaution against Kedra escaping, they lock the main gate.

Kedra continues to protest, cry, and scream.

W/o Ayda reminds her that this is an obligation.

W/o Kaltum, sensitive to Kedra's effort to escape, also tries to soothe her.

Kedra screams and shouts, "I won't be circumcised!"

Seida has prepared everything for the circumcision. She has a topaz blade for cutting, a raw chicken egg and charcoal that are mixed together and applied to the wound for healing purposes, needles made from sharp, thin, dried plants, and thin thread. She orders that Kedra be brought to her.

Kedra's little heart pounds, her breathing intensifies, and her hands shake. Her pretty little face is drenched from terror. As she continues crying, no one gives her sympathy or saves her from being circumcised.

To escape his own pain and anguish, Ato Hajji goes to a friend's home until the ceremony is over. According to culture, men are prohibited from attending the circumcision ceremony inside the house.

Ato Mustafa's wife, W/o Fatuma, holds Kedra during the circumcision. This position of honor and privilege bonds the woman and the circumcised girl for life. She sits on the chair and positions the special chair that has been prepared for Kedra. Fatuma calls for Kedra.

W/o Ayda brings Kedra, but the girl will not go without a fight. She is fighting, kicking, wiggling, struggling, and screaming. Kedra has heard about being mutilated, she is finally facing the reality of female circumcision.

W/o Fatuma tries to calm her. She looks directly into Kedra's eyes and says, "No. It is not as painful as you think. It will be over very soon."

Kedra fights back, believing she is going to die from the pain. She begs her mother not to leave her and clings desperately to her dress.

Ayda reminds her that nothing bad happened to her circumcised friends who are gathered outside. Ayda begins to take off Kedra's clothes and whispers, "Cowards die many times before their death, and you are not a coward!" After removing all of Kedra's clothes, she gives Kedra to Seida and goes into the kitchen. Ayda cannot bear to see the actual procedure. Kedra's plight brings back her own vivid memories of the extremely painful ceremony. Feeling Kedra's pain momentarily weakens her. Amina, also extremely worried by her sister's pain, begins to prepare Kedra's bed.

Outside, many children are playing on the veranda. There are more than twelve boys and girls between the ages of four and eight. Some of them are dancing and laughing, and others are silent. A few are trying to get a glimpse of Kedra's circumcision through the door.

W/o Fatuma puts Kedra on the seat that has been prepared for her.

Kedra continues crying and shouting, "Mom, help me! Mom, help me!" A small stick is forced into her mouth to stop her from crying, and she bites down on it against the pain.

Next, they tie Kedra's left leg to Fatuma's left leg and her right leg to Fatuma's right leg with belts. A young girl risks a broken or dislocated hip and/or a muscle strain if the woman holds her legs wider than the small girl's body can accommodate.

W/o Fatuma holds Kedra's hands tight around Kedra's chest and slowly opens her legs.

Kedra's face is covered with a piece of cloth to prevent her from seeing the blade or seeing herself bleeding. Kedra keeps screaming. She cries out to her father and her Mother, but nobody is there to help her.

What is going to be cut and removed is now visible for W/o Seida. Kedra is forced to endure unbearable pain. Seida, with the topaz blade in her right hand, holds Kedra's genitals to be removed with the left hand. She says, "Allah is great! Muhammad is our prophet! Allah, please dispel the devil from among us!"

Though Kedra tries with all her might to prevent them, she is powerless. Her heart is beating violently, and her screams can be heard throughout the neighborhood.

W/o Seida begins to cut out Kedra's genital organ with the topaz blade.

Kedra's horrifying scream gets louder, and the entire compound is disturbed. Calling out to her mother for help, Kedra screams in the most painfully piercing voice. Removing something so full of nerves without any form of anesthesia is extremely painful and traumatic.

On several occasions, Kedra tries to stand up and close her legs, but she cannot. Since Kedra is physically struggling, she is badly cut during the procedure and loses more blood than normal. Now hemorrhaging, she calls out for help to anyone who can hear her, but no one comes to her aid.

W/o Fatuma tries to reassure her by telling her that the procedure is finally over, but Kedra continues to cry uncontrollably. When Seida tries to remove the excess of her genital organs with her bloodied hand, the pain increases more than ever, and Kedra's screams pierce the ears of the community.

Seida is determined to remove the remaining parts, whether Kedra cries or not. For the third time, Seida removes the remaining genital tissue and throws it to the floor as though it were trash. Taking a deep breath, Seida says, "It is over!"

Kedra does not hear her. Her body covered in sweat and racked with pain. The worst part is finally over, but now she must be sewed.

Kedra's pain is getting the attention of her peers, and they stop playing, singing, and dancing on the veranda. Some of them have tears in their eyes. Everyone is silent. Most of her friends have felt the same pain and anguish. Young girls yet to be circumcised have an idea of what will happen and can imagine the pain from the descriptions of their peers.

Amina is beside herself, crying and reflecting on the pain she had to endure.

Kedra is still bleeding.

Seida, the most experienced circumciser, says, "Kedra's pain is moderate to nothing, and removing the genital ruminant is not that painful." After finishing the circumcision, Seida injects Kedra's circumcised organ and begins sewing her up.

"Please free me from this horrible suffering and pain," Kedra says, but neither parent responds. She realizes that crying is the only way to find relief from the pain she is experiencing. It is all she has left.

W/o Ayda takes the second and third snare and sews Kedra's wounded organ with thread.

Kedra is feeling extreme pain and is crying, but no one dares to go in and help her. "I am dying … please don't kill me! Help me please."

W/o Fatuma tells Kedra that it is almost over. Finally, a plastic made tube containing charcoal-rich ingredients is applied to stop the bleeding. The charcoal is thought to help the stop the bleeding and heal the wound more quickly.

Everything seems to be over, but the pain of six-year-old Kedra is not over entirely. When they uncover the veil from her face, she is sweating, and her eyes are bloodshot red. Kedra looks at her mutilated genital organ, and blood is running down her legs and dripping onto the floor. Fresh and congealed clots of blood mixed with charcoal, sand, and egg cling to her leg. The ingredient that Seida put on the wound burns. Kedra, at this age, doesn't have the capacity to grasp what has taken place, and it isn't clear to her what has been lost. The truth is that part of her body has been taken away without her consent. Nothing seems real. It is all surreal and immensely painful. Kedra stares at the lady who performed the circumcision. She's known that face and will never forget it.

They finally untie the belt on her hip and open the door. Kedra looks around at the crowd of people who allowed this injustice and bursts into tears. Some of them are quiet, and others are crying. They see the pain in her eyes and understand it. Her agonizing voice remains alive in their heads.

The mature neighbors bring butter and smear it on the top of Kedra's head. "Now she is a girl, and now she is very beautiful."

<hr>

Kedra's peers start laughing, playing, and dancing again. Her mother gives Kedra a doll, some clothes, and a watch. "Hi, my daughter, it is over. Look, there is nothing wrong with you."

Kaltum and her elder sister look at Kedra, and she bursts into tears again. When the toys are given to Kedra, she cannot hold them. She is taken to the reserved bedroom.

W/o Seida tells Kedra to sleep on her back. They tie up her legs with a rope so that she cannot move and warn her not to move for the next twenty days. During the first week, she is be prohibited to moving from her bed. If Kedra tries to urinate, the wound will open and become very painful. Therefore, she is advised not to take too much water. She is only allowed to take a sip or a spoonful of liquid after each meal.

Kedra's pain and suffering subside a bit, but she is crying angrily. Amina gives her bread, candy, and a biscuit, which are all gifts from her peers. This is considered a great ceremony for them. Until they are mature enough to understand, they must accept this procedure as a ritual and common practice that is mandatory for life in their tribe. They do not understand the crime committed on their friend.

The guests are ready to have the feast. Ato Hajji, his colleague, and others enter the room where Kedra is tied up. Mohammed and her dad look at her despairingly and try to comfort her. Her dad clears the sweat off of her forehead and leaves.

Mohammed says, "Wow, you are a real girl today!"

Amina says, "Don't say those words again. You've never known what reputation a girl has. Kedra has lost her prestige endowed by Allah. You will understand it more once you have matured."

Mohammed has been raised in a male-dominant environment and cannot understand what his sister means. He comforts Kedra but receives no response.

After attempting to make Kedra more comfortable, Amina gives her a cup of tea and a bowl of soup. Her heart is troubled with pain as she watches her sister's agony.

Invited guests take the traditionally prepared food and liquor to the guest room. Everyone has food and drink, and Kaltum serves the coffee, which is meant to end the ceremonial celebration. W/o Seida has taken three dollars from Ayda and left, telling her that she will be back next week to check on Kedra.

Mustafa and his wife, Fatuma, remain in the guest room. Some of the ladies take food into Kedra's room and express their sympathy.

Kedra is no longer crying. She tells everyone that the pain is still there—and bleeding has not ceased.

Her mother looks at it and says, "Don't worry. It is okay. It will be better soon." She adds more of the charcoal mixture to help ease the pain and minimize the bleeding. "It is only for a few days. You will be able to play just like your peers soon."

Fatuma tries to support her morale, and her sisters Kaltum and Amina are looking at her with sorrow, thinking about how much Kedra has been a victim of this tribulation and pain. They blame the agony on their parents.

Kedra is tired and tries to sleep. The blood has not stopped yet, and it has already been three solid hours since she has been circumcised. Kedra tells her mother with a fainting sound that she is feeling pain and is still bleeding.

Her mother is confused with the situation. She warns Kedra not to move and applies the mixed ingredients again.

Amina stands up quickly and says, "It has been three hours. What is wrong?"

W/o Kaltum says, "Dripping blood isn't good. If it continues like this, we have to call W/o Seida back."

Amina says, "Mom, what do you mean! Look, she is bleeding terribly. We better do something." She turns to Kedra and says, "If the bleeding continues, I will get you to the hospital—and everything will be fine."

W/o Ayda is frightened by her daughter's statement and the situation and orders Mohammed to get W/o Seida.

Mohammed hurries to get W/o Seida.

W/o Seida comes and says, "What is wrong?"

W/o Ayda says, "Kedra has not stopped bleeding!"

W/o Seida unties Kedra's legs, directs someone to get extra clothes, and ties it between her legs. She says she will come back next week.

Amina says, "If Kedra continues bleeding, we will take her to a clinic."

Shortly thereafter, the bleeding ceases—and Kedra falls asleep.

A week later, Kedra is suffering from back pain and muscle aches. She still feels the emotional effects and the vivid memories that she will never forget. Kedra remembers the people around her, her eyes being covered, the woman covering her mouth and her legs being tied. She remembers being butchered—and she remembers the pain and suffering. She is not allowed to move, and even if she wants to, her legs are tied.

Kedra has moved past the tribulations and severe pain. She is only allowed to lie on her back, leaning into a pillow for support. Whenever she tries to move, the plastic tube meant to pass urine and sewed snare would put her in an extreme pain. When Kedra feels the urge to pass urine or needs to defecate, the pain worsens. She has lost a lot of weight since she is unable to eat very much and is instructed to take in very little fluids.

W/o Seida keeps her promise and comes back a week later. She enters Kedra's bedroom without any idea of what happened to Kedra. It is her belief that the fate and health of the children she has performed circumcisions on rests on the full mandate of the Almighty. Even though she recognizes Kedra has been in pain for the entire week, her lifelong experience of circumcising girls has made her careless and complacent. W/o Seida is aware of how harmful the operation is, but it is her means of income, and she continues mutilating girls. Seida thinks that as long as she lives—if there is more infant fertility, mutilation, and circumcision— she will generate her income in this way.

W/o Seida says, "Now you are so beautiful. And is it for this much that you cried?" Seida fills Kedra's head with praise—as if her beauty came after she was butchered.

Kedra looks at her with surprise and silence. Kedra can't hear her words because all she remembers is the pain from that day. Her legs are released, and the plastic tube that troubled her while she was urinating is removed. Her legs fail to move immediately because they have been tied up all week.

Seida removes the garment by pouring water on the raw, sore organs to minimize the pain. The traditional mixture is still intact. However, it is still very painful for Kedra. She starts crying loudly because she is terrified about feeling the same anguish and pain again.

"You will feel better soon. When this is detached, it will be okay." W/o Seida slowly detaches the layered mixture of mud, charcoal, and egg, and Kedra begins to bleed again. Seida ties her legs and returns home.

Kedra is a bit relieved that the tube has been removed. However, every time she feels the need to urinate, she is forced to stand upright. Otherwise, the urine might spread all over the wound, causing burning and pain all over again. She maneuvers her body to the toilet by jumping since her legs are tied together. Kedra's appetite is improving, but she still hasn't taken in too much liquid to avoid frequent urination.

Kedra's peers have visited and try to comfort her by sympathizing with her, but Kedra believes no one understands the physical and psychological effects the circumcision has had on her. Her legs must stay tied per Seida's orders, and she is still unable to play and run as she did before.

After three agonizing weeks, Kedra's legs are finally untied. She is able to get out of bed, but she is extremely weak from the lack of movement and can barely stand. She feels lucky not to have been tied up for forty days like some of her peers. Kedra is instructed not to take long steps while she is walking to avoid reinjuring her recovering wound. If this happens, she will confront the same pain as the day of her circumcision. Thus, she is very obedient.

Her father tells her that she can go to Koran school after a month; until then, she has to stay home, recover from her wound, and eat a good diet. So far, Kedra is free of any major complications. She gradually recovers and doesn't die like some other young girls.

Kedra comes to the realization that she is a victim of female genital mutilation. It makes her angry, and she wonders why her family and the community harm her and others in this way. She has been subjected to a painful and public violation of her honor. There is no anesthetic in the operation to reduce the pain or antibiotics to fight infections.

There is no one in the family who hasn't been circumcised; the mother of this family has accomplished her duty. As a result, W/o Ayda is very well respected in the community. Their culture is respected now.

Kedra will not be disregarded as an outcast, she won't be hated by the community, and the fear of her being raped is no longer a concern. Completing the long-held tradition for all the family members, the parents believe they have done an admirable thing in preparing her and all of their children for a good family clan.

CHAPTER 3
THE AFTERMATH

Kedra has completed her primary and secondary school with satisfactory school achievements in the village of Shinile. She is the most distinguished student in her class every year. She was only sick due to the complications of her circumcision at the age of five. This year, she begins ninth grade in Dire Dawa. Her mom is extremely happy when the family moves to Dire Dawa. The city is home to many people from different nationalities and religious backgrounds; it is in the eastern part of Ethiopia.

The city is arid and extremely hot. Most men wear T-shirts, short aprons, and sandals. The women wear light pajama tops, shorts, and sandals. In the afternoon, the sun gets stronger—and residents rest or chew qat. Trains come from Addis Ababa and Djibouti. Dire Dawa is a business center, and seeing the city for the first time always amazes people. With all the people hurrying around town, it looks like a huge celebration is occurring. It's common practice to purchase and resell items controlled by the government. It is considered normal business and a very easy way to earn money. Most of the time, the city is roaring with people making business transactions. Merchants, laborers, brokers, shoe polishers, retailers, and contrabandists crowd the city. There are mini markets everywhere that sell food, clothes, perfume, stereos, and qat.

Those who come from Djibouti bring garments or perfume, and their clients and friends welcome them. A train from Addis crowds the city. A tremendous number of passengers come for leisure from the capital, Addis, and Djibouti. During May through August, thousands of Djiboutian and Christian pilgrims come to celebrate St. Gabriel. The city is crowded with visitors from Ethiopian cities and abroad. The hotels have a hard time accommodating so many visitors and renting bedrooms to the guests. Despite all the crowds, Dire Dawa does not have sanitation problems. The city was founded with the establishment of the railway and is known for its modernity and hot temperatures. It is regarded as the cleanest of all Ethiopian cities.

The citizens of Dire Dawa are ethical and usually only engage with others for income generation. Theft, temptation, and violence are nonexistent among the people of Dire Dawa. It would not be a mere exaggeration if one were to claim that most citizens in Dire Dawa are qat chewers. In the morning, everyone completes business transactions and other respective duties in a hurry to indulge in their favorite pastime of chewing qat, and the city is overcome with perfect silence. While coming down from chewing, most people are depressed, and a few people become frightened.

In the city, residents from many tribal and religious backgrounds live in full harmony and compromise. The Somali, Oromo, Guraghe, and Amhara live with full freedom and reflect their respective customs, traditional dishes, and other traditions. It is a custom to go out for what a wake when the sun sets. Christians gather in their churches, and Muslims gather in their mosques to worship, pray, and celebrate their religions. The Muslim community celebrates Eid Alfeter, Eid aladha, or Mewlid, and the Christians celebrate Easter, Christmas, or Epiphany. Everyone wishes one another good wishes, and the city is bright and decorated. Every religious person celebrates the New Year (Inkutatash) together, wishes Happy New Year to each other, and expresses wishes of happiness, peace, prosperity, and health. Dire Dawa has many destitute villages with miserable living standards.

Kedra's friend's mother, W/O Medina, works in a variety of roles from dawn until night. She wakes up in the morning and sells fruit and bread on the side of her house. Soraya helps her mother after school. Her duties include preparing and serving tea to customers. She speaks about her disappointment and frustration of having a very poor life.

Kedra's family purchased a house in the beloved city of Dire Dawa and operates a café in the city. She and Soraya often study together. Soraya grew up in Dire Dawa, in a village named Hafetesa, and she is one of six children. Her dad has retired from the Djibouti railway.

Soraya is academically poor, but she has improved her grades since becoming friends with Kedra, who has basic knowledge of almost every subject. Kedra is improving her basic English despite the shackles of poverty and gender. In doing so, they read books and newspapers in English, and they listen to English music. If they find difficult words, they look them up in the dictionary.

Kedra is the most outstanding student in her class. Moreover, Kedra is assigned to help slow learners in the class by her teacher. With no reservation, Kedra demonstrates basic skills in English, which helps her understand most subjects without difficulty.

Kedra and Soraya both respect their religion, have strong motivation for academics, and have spent much anguish and suffering in their childhoods. Kedra supports Soraya by buying her clothes, shoes, and cosmetics from what is given to her from her parents. She also gives her money to support her health through traditional medicine. Because of their bond, people think they're sisters. Kedra has bright hopes and dreams for her education, but that is not supported by her mother. Unsympathetic replies are given when studying is held at a higher value than the work at the café. Kedra continues to study hard, but the thought of how much time she spent in and out of the hospital and in bed after her genital mutilation still haunts her.

In her mother's opinion, a girl should not complete more than twelve grades, but her father has a different outlook. "If anyone from whatever age level proposes Kedra to marriage, she will marry and not complete school. So, her going to school is worthless," exclaims her dad. Her parents believe that the essence of education is only for securing a job rather than knowledge. More importantly, they also believe that a boy should go to college to find a job to earn money that will help him support his family, and a girl should respect her marriage, treat her husband, give birth, and raise her children. From this perspective, Ayda says, "Kedra, you should not give me such silly reasons not to serve in the café. If you wish, you can study now because you have no work right now. Sit down and study. Your friend Soraya is busy helping her parents; despite this, even she is improving her grades. So, what is wrong with you?"

Kedra's father Hajji says, "You are behaving differently. I don't know where this is coming from. Are you complaining about working as if you are going to be a smart student?"

Kedra begins to realize that her parents' mentality of her going to college is a blessing that is only endowed for boys. She goes to her room without any comments. She takes some time to understand the gap that is being created between her parents and herself. It is not only attributed to her being a girl; it is the influence of a male-dominant society. Kedra's older sister, Amina, and her stepsisters born from W/o Kaltum have also been victims of this outlook. They will be proposed to for marriage before completing their high school studies, but the boys in the family have already completed their higher secondary school education. On the contrary, Kedra wants to prove her equality to the opposite sex and feels a strong urge to continue her education. Therefore, she changes her study schedule, does homework in her free time at the café, reads books in English, eats her dinner early, goes to her room, and studies. She also studies on Saturday and Sunday nights with Soraya because tenth grade is hard.

Kedra has another friend and classmate named Atum Indris. Atum was born and raised in Dire Dawa, but she spends her leisure time in Djibouti. Her mother departed from her when she was eight years old, and her father is living with his two wives in Jijiga town. She is fast and very good at her job. Atum has grown up with a great deal of freedom and is living with her sister in a village called Ashewa.

Kedra and Soraya start helping Atum with her studies because she is a poor student, and as a result, she has improved her learning abilities. The three of them are really good friends, and they often describe fantasies about their future womanhood and past tribulations or pain of growing up as a young girl in a male-dominant society.

Atum never stops telling them about her boyfriend in Djibouti. Ismael Deria is her first boyfriend, and he comes weekly to Dire Dawa to meet her. He sometimes brings commodities from Djibouti to distribute to merchants in Dire Dawa. The fact that he is decent, good boy, is the owner of a huge property, and is in his early twenties is enough for Atum. Atum's parents are often away from home, and she is able to spend time with her boyfriend. The death of her mother is still painful, and she spends a lot of romantic time with her boyfriend because she believes it will take her mind off of the pain.

Kedra and Soraya are still suffering from their parents' conservative concerns, and they tell Atum to carry on with her romantic life. The fact that Atum is following the same religious faith and identical ethnicity gives them a chance to analyze their lives meticulously.

Soraya is not in good health. She was circumcised and sewed when she was a five-year-old child. There was a lot of bleeding, and her urethra was wrongly sewed together with another part of her genital organ. This action prevented her from urinating for four solid days, and her kidneys became infected due to the excess liquid, which led to severe pain and fever. Soraya was on the verge of death, but her relatives and family raised money to afford care at Ethio-Djibouti Railway Hospital in Dire Dawa.

The doctors opened the sewed genital organs in hopes that her quality of life could be better after surgery. However, with her parents' conservative outlook and the customs and culture of the society, her genitals were sewed again. She frequently suffers from kidney infections and severe pain during menstruation—even though the surgery was supposed to make things better. Soraya's family is poor, and some of their relatives help them when she is seriously sick. Recently, Kedra and Atum tried to help her. Her friends sympathize with her and know the pain she must endure. Kedra is concerned with the pain of her beloved friend and says, "This health disorder and anguish are attributed due to conservative faith and stigmatized culture. It is a pity. Let God tell us the days that all these miseries will be over."

Atum says, "I feel like we girls are created disguised and cursed. I don't really know why God is punishing women on earth instead of hell for every sin that humankind has committed. It encourages one to ask, 'Is this hell on earth?' If the tribulation and misery in hell is more than what we are confronted with on earth, hell is the absolute place for punishment."

Kedra says, "Don't say that. We are not cursed. We are not born or created to be cursed. Even our parents are not doing this to hurt us; rather, it is due to a lack of awareness. In their perception, they are doing it for our good."

Soraya digests her friend's comment and says, "I agree with Kedra's idea. We girls have got family and cultural influence that impede us. We are not given the same privileges as our sex partners—males—and we are expected to serve in the kitchen. The necessary support is not given to us. Thus, we can't take school seriously and appropriately. We will never know what the Koran says if we are not literate. Thus, we will be in a position to accept and believe what has been told to us. Look, my dad thinks that education is worthless for me as well as for my elder sisters. He also believes that a girl's fate is solely limited to marriage, engagement, giving birth, and raising children. Our mothers, since they are not educated, have long accepted these rituals and customs their whole lives, and they perceive it as a word from God. This is why they are stigmatized to this backward culture and want us to follow false ritualistic teachings. For example, now there is nothing that we can decide for our own bodies. The three of us were circumcised in childhood, and we are all suffering from its complications."

After a few moments of silence, Kedra says, "Those girls whom circumcision and sewing are not their culture are privileged and have freedom to practice safe sex and be engaged in a legal marriage."

Atum takes a bite from her cake and says, "What is worst is the fact that all these backward traditions are committed to us by women. Yet, our women strongly urge, argue, and insist on the continuation this horrible practice."

Soraya says, "I am jealous of those girls who are not circumcised, sewed, and victims of a backward culture. They succeed in their academics, professional lives, and marriages. We are not even lucky enough to find our loved ones by ourselves. There is no sense in regretting the past; what is worthy is to be ready for the future. Human well-being must be a factor to be valued and respected—and not being victims of this practice. We have to prove that we are not inferior to our male partners."

They stand up and return home.

CHAPTER 4

BORN TO SUFFER

Soraya feels a sudden rush of extreme pain, and she tries to get relief by holding her waist tightly with both hands. Her mother is bothered by Soraya's illness and makes her take traditional medication. However, after a dreadful night filled with pain, she doesn't feel better in the morning. She is taken to the railway hospital.

The doctor says, "As a result of your circumcision and sewing, performed thirteen years ago, an accumulation of blood intended for release during your menstrual flow has accumulated in your womb. This is the reason for the discomfort and pain."

Soraya and her mother look at each other, and her mother says, "This is a mistake we committed. My daughter has been suffering through life because of our wrong deeds. Had it not been for the funds raised by our relatives and neighbors several times, she would have died."

The doctor says, "If you agree to admit Soraya, first, we would give her medication through her blood vessels. After six hours, the medication would cause the blood to pour out of her womb. If you agree to open her sewed genital organ, she will receive permanent relief. If Soraya returns home, her case may become more complicated. If you agree to this idea, you can confirm with your signature." He goes back into his office.

W/o Medina takes a step toward her daughter Soraya and gazes at her with a complete silence. She is conflicted internally, but she has to choose either her daughter's health by reopening her genitals or confronting the long-held societal constraints. It is a difficult decision.

Ato Kamil e comes to the hospital, and W/o Medina tells him everything the doctor told her to do to help improve Soraya's health. Unfortunately, Ato Kamil refuses and will not take it into consideration.

"Soraya is at an age at which she should be engaged in marriage and be giving birth. We would become outcasts in society if her genitals are opened, and there will be no one to propose to her for marriage."

There are families who associate girls' circumcisions with economic benefits in some instances. If one is circumcised and sewed, she is perceived to be a virgin—and the bridegroom's side will offer ransom money or property. Therefore, a girl's circumcision is counted as a financial benefit to her parents, and Soraya's family lives in miserable, impoverished conditions. In their mind-set, reopening the genital organ could cause them to miss the opportunity for financial prosperity. They believe that no clan would pay good money for Soraya if her genitals are reopened. From the male's prospective, there are no privileges in finding true love. In this culture, marriages are not based on pure love. For this reason, the wife is treated as common house property, and in the eyes of Soraya's family, it doesn't matter as long as they gain financial freedom.

The nurse brings an intravenous solution, dilutes it, and injects it.

After lunch, the doctor comes back.

Soraya is feeling a little better.

The doctor looks at the parents and asks, "Have you decided now?"

Soraya's father stands and says, "For the time being, you better give her the medication. According to our culture, no one will marry a girl who is not circumcised and sewed. Women could commit intercourse before marriage and result in pregnancy. We don't want this for our daughter."

The doctor says, "What was performed on Soraya many years ago will permanently stay with her and only to make her sicker." The doctor is not convinced by the traditional and cultural reasons that Soraya's parents gave. Since they are from different religions, cultures, and ethnic backgrounds, they do not reach a consensus easily. The doctor says, "To prevent the infection from spreading, medicine is injected and given through her blood vessel. After a few minutes, the blood accumulated in her uterus and womb will be cleaned and drained. As I have told you, this is not a permanent solution for her problem." He leaves the room.

Soraya is annoyed and surprised with her parents' stubborn beliefs and stares at them in silence. She understands what will happen if she does not have the surgery to reopen her genitals: death. Her parents are not sympathetic or even concerned with the possibility of death. She feels frustrated and hopeless because money is worth much more to her parents than their daughter's life.

Soraya's parents go out of the room to discuss the situation with a friend.

Kedra says, "Our tribulation and torment have been unlimited. Our parents and males primarily determine our existence in this universe. We have no fortune and power. Our God forgot us. Nobody recognizes our utterance. Every trouble has been given only to us. Is it a crime to be a female?" She bites her lips. "Being a female is not a crime. God created us like all the other females in the world without losing anything. We should not grumble with God, and it would be unfair to grumble with God because human beings committed sins or crimes. Anyway, let God save our health. Let our God give us tolerance and patience. All these tribulations may be resolved one day. We should pray for this day."

Kedra's parents are silent and stand with their heads down for a number of minutes.

Soraya is rolled back to her room on a stretcher. Even though Kedra and Atum feel the need to spend the night with her, they cannot because of their family's constraints. They bid her good night and return home.

The next day, Soraya is feeling better. Her fever is lower, she can walk and eat, and she seems well enough to go home. Soraya is happy her pain is gone, and she is smiling and laughing with her peers. She overhears the doctor saying that her current freedom from pain may not last very long. He is very happy that the pain is gone, but this particular incident may not be isolated. If he opens the circumcised genital organ, he might face criminal charges or personal attacks from her parents. To avoid this, he accepts their unorthodox reasons for wanting Soraya's genitals to remain sewed.

He turns to her parents and says, "As you see, today her health has improved. It appears safe to leave the hospital. The pain has ceased, the fever has been regulated, and she is eating again."

Soraya remains in the hospital for three more days, Soraya knows that if she doesn't get medication regularly, she could become sick again. She has always helped her parents, but her contributions do not receive any credit. Soraya is offended by her parents because they only think about themselves and focus on the advantages they may gain from her marrying. She feels a deep sadness.

CHAPTER 5

KEDRA MEETS LOVE

Kedra keeps working in her parents' coffee shop. There has been an increase in the number of customers, and the amount of staff is limited. It is Wednesday, Kedra has begun to serve the customers. Her hands and feet have a lovely tattooed design that attracts customers. Kedra covers her hair and ears with a headscarf, according to her cultural beliefs and customs.

A young man who lives on the Ashewa block, Ateib Abdullahi, frequents the coffee shop each morning before work. Today, he is filled with commodities and ornaments to sell to the retailers in the city. He was raised in a poor environment and is currently making money through trade. He has traded bread, goats, and many other commodities that are on the contraband list of Djibouti and Somalia for a handsome profit. From the profits, he opened barber shop in Dire Dawa to help his parents. Currently, he has been purchasing goods from Jijiga and reselling them in Dire Dawa. His work ethic, hard work, and good personality have made him recognized, respected, and favored by his parents, relatives, and neighbors.

Ateib notices Kedra in the coffee shop in a way a boy likes a girl for the first time. This is not the only time he has noticed Kedra, but this time, he sees her Kedra differently. She is remarkably different from the girl he first saw. She has somehow changed. She is gorgeous, and in a different light, she is more attractive. He is drawn to her quality. Her lips are sharp, and her round eyes capture his attention as he looks at her.

Kedra is from the Somalia nationality too, but they are from different clans. Kedra is from Hawe, and Ateib is from the clan of Darood. Both are followers of Islam.

Kedra walks over to his table and says, "What shall be ordered?"

Ateib tries to control his inner thoughts, rolls his eyes, and looks her up and down. Even though she is fully covered, he is intrigued. His heart starts to beat faster and louder and urges him to behave inappropriately. Kedra senses what he wants from her, and she asks again what he wants from the snack bar.

Ateib apologizes and orders. He is drawn in by the way she walks. At that moment, she exudes her femininity. It is not possible to completely recognize her quality because her hair is covered, but she is pretty and has a good personality. Ateib thinks, *Doesn't she reflect a certain quality? What type of person is she? I am dumbfounded that I can't fully observe her.* Ateib is surprised at these questions because he hadn't recognized her beauty before.

Kedra is discombobulated by his interest and questions his motives. She asks other waitresses to take out his breakfast and sits down. She starts to see him engage with emotion. His eyes are focused on her, and she can feel his heart longing for her.

After finishing his breakfast, he stands up, puts his hands in his pocket, and walks toward Kedra to pay. That Friday morning is unique for him because he usually pays at the table, but he is so impressed by her that he wants to pay her specifically.

She starts fixing her headscarf with her trembling hands.

Ateib removes his hands from his pocket to pay the bill. "Today, you are looking very smart and more beautiful than usual. I can't see your hair or other parts, but you seem quite attractive. I am surprised. I should have been impressed by your quality before now."

She is under much distress. It is shocking to hear such utterances from a young man she hadn't had the pleasure of experiencing until now, but she is a bit annoyed and is unable to speak. Kedra takes the money, counts out his change, puts it on the counter, and stretches out her beautifully tattooed hands.

Ateib tries to control his emotions, and takes out a perfume bottle from a plastic container and asks her to accept it.

She accepts nervously and asks, "What shall I do with it?"

"You have become very attractive, beautiful, and glittered. It is a reflection of my admiration for you. I want you to have this. I give you this perfume as a reward."

Kedra is skeptical of accepting the perfume, but she is very touched by his gift. She is speechless and nervous. She says, "Thank you. The perfume is very nice and one of the best, but I don't need it. Please take it back."

"Never mind! It is nothing. You will like it when you smell it once more. Even if you hate it, this is my gift. This is minor for you—who are inspired of quality and gorgeous. So, please accept it." He shows her other perfumes and says, "Look! I have also this type." He is beginning to sweat.

"Never! Absolutely not. I don't need it," says Kedra.

Ateib says, "I have two of them—and let it be with you. Take whatever you like. It is because I have perceived you as attractive rather than usual." He walks away.

Even though Kedra likes the perfumes, she is disappointed by the insinuation. She can breathe better when he leaves. Kedra is astonished at all of the emotions she feels running so chaotically inside. It is he who impressed and challenged her from the time they met.

When Ateib escapes from the snack bar, Kedra is shocked and is unable to talk. She starts smelling the perfumes. This is the first time she has received personal attention from the opposite sex. She continues smelling them. They have an interesting flavor, and they are popular in the market. She has no close friends to tell about her morning. She worries about their clan difference and her parents' strict control over her. Her relationship with the opposite sex will be an issue for her parents.

Ateib is quiet and shy. He is surprised that he expressed his interest to her. In that instance he recognizes that there is so much time dedicated to finding girlfriends. His motive is clear, and he emanates feelings of true love. While his heartbeat is still increased, and he is drenched with sweat. He goes to work, but all he can think about is Kedra. When Ateib sees other women in the street, Kedra's reflection overpowers them. He assumes he will see her in the morning and begins to daydream about her glittered lips and eyes. His mind is flooded with thoughts about the differences in their clans. Clan differences are not a simple matter—even though they share the same nation, religion, and language. Ateib quickly dismisses it from his mind because he is inspired by his love for her.

That night is too long for him. He can't wait to see Kedra in the morning. It seems like a longer night than usual, and he counts the hours until he will see her again. Despite his failed attempt to impress her with the perfume, Ateib returns after lunch the next day. Kedra is not there. A mature woman, Kedra's mother, is behind the snack bar. He is offended and dismayed that she is not there. He sits on one of the chairs, orders a

Coca-Cola, and waits for Kedra. He stares at the door and hopes to see her come in. Two hours passed with no sign of Kedra. He pays for his drink, returns to his job, and hopes he will see her the next day.

After winding up her daily lesson, Kedra and Atum go to visit Soraya. She was discharged from the hospital the day before. They go into her bedroom, and she shares the details from her hospital stay and explains what the physician said to her parents.

Atum notices the absence of Soraya's parents and says, "If I were you, I would have my sewed genital organs reopened for the sake of my future health, but it must be done in secret."

Soraya thinks it is impossible to do that without her parents knowing. "If my parents are informed—or if someone wants to marry me—and realizes that my genital organs are not sewed, they will think I have already been in a sexual relationship with someone. You know? I will be in risk, and in a big problem."

Atum says, "Would it be better to be in pain and anguish by disease until a husband comes for you? You will not recover your health, you'll feel unsafe, you will have incurable health problems, and your health will remain at risk."

Kedra says, "It is a hard decision, but a person who is going to marry you may not come soon enough. It might be five or ten years. If you want to progress in your education and help your parents, you can't get married in such short period of time. In fact, the decision to marry or not to marry is not our decision; it is our parents' decision. You will not know when it happens because only God knows when it will happen. So, you plan your future—if you survive. The decision should be yours to make. I agree with the idea of Atum."

Soraya considers her friend's advice and feels nervous. She can't see any way out of the long-held tradition. She could make the decision to reopen her sewed genital organ and be relieved of pain and possible infection or accept these disparities; otherwise, she might die. This is challenging for her, and it is beyond her capacity as a minor. If she had an opportunity to choose who she would marry, she would make the decision to open her sewed genital organ. Nevertheless, on the basis of social culture, her parents will negotiate her marriage. She will be given for marriage regardless of her interest for anyone—as long as the dowry is large enough. Soraya is despondent and cannot decide her fate—even with the encouragement of her friends. Her friends understand her problem and urge her to tell her doctor, listen to her body, and then decide.

Atum says, "Nothing is more important than your health. In order to survive in this world, you should realize your existence for it is the so-called life. Even if human beings are obstacles for the privileges we get from God, you should enjoy even with little happiness. Although human beings are guilty of creating this backward culture and old customs, we should save ourselves from death and realize our existence. If the physician's decision is to open the sewed organ, do it. If your parents impose any problems, you will live with me or go to Djibouti where my sister has lived!"

Atum and her two friends had the procedure performed at an early age. Atum's mother died, and she is estranged from her father. It is easy for her to decide. She had her boyfriend open a clinic in Djibouti in secret.

Ateib endures be a never-ending night and thinks of Kedra and his desire to be with her. He gets up early and goes to the snack bar to profess his infatuation for her.

Kedra is sitting on the counter.

He greets her with warm heartfelt gestures that reflect his true emotions.

Kedra is uncomfortable and scans the room to see if people are watching. Kedra reacts with the her guarded, shy greeting and pulls her headscarf up tightly.

He is speechless, reserved, and unable to profess his true feelings.

Kedra looks at him daringly.

Ateib says, "I couldn't tell you what I felt and have in mind so far about you. Perhaps I want to know whether you feel the emotion of love after I tell you my internal feelings. Even if I have decided to tell you what I have felt in front of you by observing your eyes and body, I lack words to express my motive. If I make you mine, I will consider you a reward given from God. It will happen in a day—mine is a true love. Let me tell you from the bottom of my heart. From the very start of yesterday morning, my mind has been thinking of you. As you have seen today, I came very early. I believe we have known each other long ago. Perhaps my heart might have approached yours; my love might have fallen to yours. I couldn't recognize your love consciously. Your beauty is glittering from day to day, and your stylistic appearance is increasing."

Kedra listens to him attentively, and his words cause her to think about his proposition. She is awestruck by his request, and her heart is beating so fast.

"I am not here to eat. I am here to express my intention of having a love affair."

Ateib's words challenge her love brain to flourish, and Kedra says, "I understand what you are saying to me, but this is not a simple issue for me." She stands up.

Ateib says, "Please, even if we have known each other for a short period of time, my feelings are not trivial." Ateib thinks Kedra is acting like a young girl who sometimes says one thing but wants another.

She looks at the customers around her and asks him quietly to step aside. "First of all, I am not ready for a love affair. My age is under twenty, and I have a long prospect and aspiration; my education is my priority. Furthermore, we know how our parents perceive love affairs before marriage."

Ateib says, "You don't need to tell me that you are kid. Many females who are thirteen and fourteen are married and have children, but this doesn't mean you should be like the others. You will be mature. My intention is not to marry you very soon. I realize that our culture, religion, and parents' attitudes are harsh. Our love affair will not create a problem with your education. You can learn and may become whatever you wish. I need it from you."

Kedra replies, "I know that you will never marry me—even if you wish. I am telling you that I am not ready for this sort of relationship with the opposite sex. In addition, even though others have gotten married at thirteen and fourteen, I shouldn't do it. So, you don't need to tell me about other people as an example. Even if we were from the same religion and culture, we are from different clans—and that creates a large gap. My parents keep and follow the regulations of the clan strictly."

In Somalia, for those who want to be married, the clan background needs to have profound credit. This is one of the key issues to be realized before a marriage is undertaken. If the couple is from the same clan, they receive privileges and advantages without being far from their surroundings. They can defeat any enemy from other clans without feeling loneliness and seclusion from their clan. This rule is especially pertinent in rural areas, but in urban areas, people have married without complying to this regulation.

If a marriage occurs between members of different clans, the parents need a guarantee for the security of their children. In a rural community, if the female or male misses their clan, they will be considered deserters. In addition, they will be considered recent arrivals for the clan they join; hence, they are unable to gain appropriate support. Consequently, even if there are people who have been married from different clans, society prefers them to be married within their own clan. To avoid this problem, parents teach their children about which clan they come from, and every member of society is responsible for knowing the relationships that extend from ten to twenty different kinship systems.

Kedra tells Ateib about their disparity in clans.

Ateib replies, "The issue you raised is not that simple. If we cooperate with each other and believe in strong love, the difference in clan doesn't matter. We are from the same nationality and religion. Our blood is red. Our appearance is black. We have two eyes and two legs like other human beings. We are different only in attitude, appearance, and sex. If you receive love from me, and vice versa, this is the fundamental issue. You will get experience if you practice love."

By proposing a solution for the problem, they might face it courageously.

Kedra is surprised by his courage and says, "Please! I am at work. If my parents come, it will not be good for me." She pounds the counter with her hands and begs him to leave.

Ateib's heart is filled with happiness. "Anyway, I will come again when your work is over. Please take my intention in to account."

Kedra accepts his respect, puts her hand on her chest, and picks up the perfumes. "They are good and flavorful perfumes." She smiles and thanks him.

Ateib says, "I have more. I will bring the perfume to you with great happiness." As he leaves, he bids her goodbye.

The concept of saying "I love you" is difficult for Kedra, but she is surprised by his drive. Kedra considers him a courageous man whose mind is set on getting his way, but it might be true love. She takes a few deep breaths, and her heart begins to race Sometimes she giggles, and other times, she is surprised and somewhat annoyed with the thought of being in love with Ateib.

Kedra's mind is preoccupied and not focused on accurately counting money that is being paid to the café. She is assisting people when other waitresses are missing or busy, even if it is a market day, and she stops on occasion to think of Ateib.

After professing his interest and his motives to her when he looked her in the eyes and scanned her beautiful face, Ateib hopes she will be in favor of him—even if she didn't reflect a sign of approval.

Kedra returns from school one day during the week and stops by her sister's house. On Friday and Saturday, Kedra tells Amina about her interaction with Ateib and his request to have a love affair. Kedra shares the problems she might face if she decides she wants to be involved with Ateib.

Amina says, "What does it matter? You reflect happiness at the thought of loving him. You should expect that someone else might love you once in your life. By the way, who is he? Do I know him?"

Kedra replies, "He is called Ateib. I don't think you know him. We share the same ethnicity and religion, but he is from a different clan. He is a member of Darood and is a trader in the market. Being in different clans is not simple for our parents. They prefer categorizing people in terms of clan, race, and religion."

"What is your response to him?" Amina asks.

"Actually, I didn't give him any promise or hope. I was cold, but his speech showed me that he might be from a good family, and he seems innocent and in love. I was shocked, but I couldn't express it in words. After our meeting, I recalled the time he first came to the market, and my memory urged my eyes to look at him."

Amina says, "This sort of feeling should cause you to approach him. To love is good. You are chanceful. As you know, I got married by our parents' decision. However, love cannot exist in a short period of time. First of all, somebody will look at your body, appearance, posture, and quality and then love you. Next, when you are introduced to each other cordially and start to live respectfully, you feel unconscious, which is a difficult state, but it can be changed through love."

"Love can't exist within a short period of time, but if he loves me, I don't know what I will do. You know how our parents are. I feel they will cut me up into small strips."

Amina says, "Anyway, don't worry. There is a God. God knows if you love him without controlling your senses, you can do nothing. If this happens, you should forget the clan difference between you and any problems you might face due to this. You should tolerate and carry on with the person you love. I will agree with the decision you make."

Kedra returns home after speaking with her sister, eats dinner, and goes to bed. She starts to worry about expressing her love for Ateib confidently. She is eager to see him in the morning.

CHAPTER 6

A BREWING LOVE AFFAIR

The day is extremely hot in Dire Dawa, and the snack bar has a lot of customers. Kedra sits down on the counter and wait for Ateib, hoping he will visit again. Fortunately, while Kedra is attending to the costumers, he enters the snack bar. She is very happy and giggles in delight.

He approaches her and asks, "Did you pass the night safely?"

Kedra is lost in thought and says, "Thanks to God!" She returns to her seat and attempts to control her emotions.

"You seem to be busy today," Ateib says.

"Yes, we are busy," she says.

"Let me help you," he says, and he starts assisting the customers.

Kedra quietly observes him from the counter. As the customers decrease, she asks him to rest and eat.

"Today is Friday. Two weeks have passed since I expressed my love for you. I'm not here to eat or drink tea, but merely to see you and express my love to you. I have expressed my interest and ambition, and you should clearly understand how I feel." Ateib looks into her eyes.

Kedra begins to feel a plethora of emotions she can't explain. She looks nervously at the floor, the door, and at Ateib. While she wants to reflect the love she feels for him, she feels uncomfortable. She looks left and right and finally says, "Please! I am worried. You know every problem we have. I've explained how my parents would feel. Must I explain again?"

Ateib says, "I know that you say you are a mature girl, but neither your father nor mother will marry you. On the contrary, they will give you to a husband when you mature—but you won't know or love him. Are you trying to say you have other friends you are interested in?

"I don't have a boyfriend—if that is what you're asking," Kedra says. She agrees that it should be a mutual agreement.

Ateib asks, "Where is your destiny after this—or will you wait until you are old to realize your fate? Anyway, I love you from the bottom of my heart. I realize you will love me one day. When we live together in love, you might even regret that you have missed me thus far."

Kedra is impressed by his speech, and once she looks into his eyes and then his stretched-out hands extended over the counter, she says, "What you are saying might be true. God knows it," says Kedra with a playful tone. While she is leaning toward the door, Kedra and her father see each other. She is annoyed.

Ateib doesn't recognize her father at first, but he stands up after he sees her eyes. She tells him that it is her father as her father reaches her. He looks at Ateib, and then he looks at Kedra and nonchalantly asks about the job.

Ateib understands the behavior of her father, takes money from his pocket, and pays Kedra without even eating anything. Kedra recognizes his cleverness, accept his money, and gives him his change.

After school the next day, Atum and Kedra go to Soraya's house.

Soraya says she was thinking of them today at her doctor's appointment.

Kedra asks. "How are you? What did the physician tell you? What is the result of the investigation?"

"The physician tells me that the circumcision and sewed has affected my urethra. I also have a kidney stone that could cause problems during menstruation. He says my urine can't expel, which causes me to be seriously ill. The physician ordered medicine to help me get well."

"So, what is the solution? Did he tell you? If you have kidney stones, do you need to be operated on?"

Soraya says, "The kidney stone is too small, and the doctor tells me it might be expelled through urine. However, one of my kidneys has been hurt, and that is what is causing my pain. The last solution is to open my sewed genital organ, but the physician can't open it without the permission of my parents."

Kedra sits down on a chair and asks, "What will you decide? Have you explained this to your parents?"

Atum says, "How do you explain this to your parents?"

"In the hospital, they disapproved and showed their disagreement with their signatures. The solution proposed by the physician is unacceptable. I don't think they will change their minds."

Kedra says, "Anyway, tell them what the physician explained to you. If they agree with that, perhaps they will approve of having the sewed organ reopened. If they do not agree this time around, as we said before, you need to go to the clinic secretly and have it reopened." Her eyes fill with tears. "Your parents do not care about your health problem as long as you walk properly or are constantly sick and lying in bed. Can't they see that the disease is really hurting you? If you are determined, you should have the sewed genital organ opened as recommended by the physician—even if your parents do not allow it. This should be done at the expense of other alternatives."

Soraya understands that her friend's advice is for her own sake and is related to her family's reputation in the community. If the sewed genital organ is reopened, her parents would think she had a sexual affair with someone before marriage. She is worried that her parents will severely beat her, curse her, and remove her from the house.

Her friends feel like they are experiencing the same agony, and they urge her to listen to the physician to help improve her quality of life.

Atum says, "When you were a child, you became a victim of this backward culture. I don't why you ask your parents to make decisions concerning your life. You are mature enough in age and attitude. Furthermore, as you know and hear, many females get their sewed genital organs opened in secret when they need to enjoy their sex lives with their lovers. When they are mature for marriage, they have it sewed again. Being circumcised and sewed doesn't always prevent females from having sexual intercourse when they fall in love. Yours is not for this purpose; instead, your goal is to save your life, which has been given to you by God. This is not a crime according to the Koran and non-Eastern traditions."

Kedra and Atum try to convince her, but Soraya is worried and struggles with listening to her parents or having her organs secretly reopened. She is scared and tells them that she plans to open her sewed organs and not tell her parents.

Atum says, "Soraya, your decision is what matters the most, and it should come before your parents' decision. It is possible to have the procedure done secretly in a clinic. The clinic has nothing to make you feel scared, and there is no extra space for your parents."

Kedra says, "Our intention is for your sake. We are not forcing you to go against your parents; we are advising you. We don't feel the same discomfort as you feel."

Soraya's friends are happy she is taking a stand and choosing to improve her quality of life. They agree to take her to the clinic on Saturday.

Kedra says, "We know the impact of this backward custom and our parents. If I were facing your problem, there would be no other reason than to lead me toward death for the sake of my parents' respect."

Atum laughs and goes to the door. "Your problem is due to poor health. My problem is different because I want to enjoy sexual activity with my boyfriend. I had my sewed genital organ opened to accommodate that." Atum admits this for the first time.

Kedra and Soraya are amazed and surprised and appreciate her courage. They had heard that some teens had their sewed genital organs opened for the sole purpose of engaging in sexual intercourse, but they hadn't realized that was the case for Atum.

Atum sees the shocked look on the girls' faces and says, "Why would I lie? What I said is true. When Hassan and I were introduced, we fell in love and engaged in an immensely true and strong love affair. We had to see each other every day. When the Djibouti sun set at five o'clock, he would wait for me at school. We would go to town to discuss our love situation deeply and for a long period of time. I felt a pleasant atmosphere from the warm air breathed from his lungs as I gave him true love from the bottom of my heart. In return, he gave me true love from the bottom of his heart.

"In 1988, at the end of Ramadan, he and I went to the Sheraton in Djibouti and rested there. We really enjoyed each other and had a really good time. We are extremely happy, excited, and in love. My sister is really surprised by our love affair. With great love and compatibility, we had such a good time. Since I am a human, my emotions are challenged by his love. I simply understand that Hassan feels the same way. Even though we passed about eight months in love, I didn't dare to have sex with him. I try to practice sex and give my virginity to Hassan—who I still love very much—but it has been difficult. We are in an unpleasant situation because I am circumcised and sewed.

"Even if we were enjoying the Ramadan ceremony together, we felt inconvenient since we failed to do something important. Our motive was too warm, and we were sweating. Our heartbeats were violent and nervous. We were chewing qat in the bedroom of the hotel. We looked at each other, and he kissed me. I was inspired by a special motive, which I hadn't experienced before. It was new for me. I was shocked."

Kedra is listening to Atum attentively. *Atum is the only person who talks about being lonely in her bedroom.*

"When we left the hotel, I went home. I was filled with such pain because we couldn't have sex for the first time. I blamed my dead mother and father for being the reason for us not having sex that day. I felt harsh and inconvenienced because of my body and the impact it had on my sexual affair. I secretly went to Djibouti and had my sewed genital organ opened in a private clinic."

Soraya says, "Is your sewed genital organ opened? Do you have sex with your boyfriend?"

Kedra and Soraya are surprised and fascinated because Atum's story sounds so adventurous.

Atum says, "There is no reason for me to lie. I am telling the truth. My boyfriend, Hassen, was not initially informed of my decision. A week after the Ramadan fast, I was totally devoted to Hassen. When I gave him my virginity, he was very surprised. He admired my courage. You will not consider sexual intercourse a big issue as long as you fall in true love because the intimacy is what's important. Sex is considered a bad practice before marriage in our culture and to our parents, but it is not bad. If we practice it properly, the pleasure of sex is quite exciting— among all gifts of God. This experience is what you fail to do earlier in life. Even though I realize the satisfaction gained from sex is interesting, I regret waiting until I turned fifteen like females in other countries."

Soraya stands up and says, "I appreciate your courage, but I don't think I will have sex before marriage. It is against God's will."

Kedra says, "I don't have that type of problem. Your mother passed, and you're far away from your father. You feel free and do whatever you wish—and entertain your lover. However, Soraya and I are not as fortunate with the existence of our parents and their considerations of our culture as appropriate customs and their control over us,"

Atum says, "Think about it! Since we are created as human beings, to love is God's gift to us. It is the most exciting and precious gift. Unless we are informed and experience love on our own, we face the same problems that thousands and millions have faced before us. We face marriage without love, sex without love, birth without love, and life without love. We will be married to a person we don't love and give birth to several children out of obligation and not love. Hence, we will be housewives and slaves to our household chores. Our destinies will be in the kitchen. Due to cultural influences, we fail to think with our conscious minds. Since we can't speak about our rights, we simply eat and drink with no voice."

Soraya asks, "For the sake of your lover, you opened the sewed genital organ. What will you do if he doesn't marry you?"

"Hassen tells me that he loves me. I believe him. I don't think he will fall in love with someone else. If it's God's will, we will get married. If we cannot get married, it depends on the will of God. I can do nothing without sadness, but I can achieve entertainment, happiness, and the satisfaction gained from sex at this point. Even though I feel sad because I lost my mother, I will not regret passing through this life this way—and I don't predict that I will lose my boyfriend."

On Saturday, Atum takes Soraya to a clinic in town. After her mutilated and sewed genital organ is opened in secret, she returns home. The vaginal reopening is not a big operation, especially since anesthesia is involved. Females are not subject to severe pain and suffering as much as they are when it is sewed as a child. However, according to the families of this culture, it is unimaginable to think that millions of women who are victims of this backward culture could get this opportunity for vaginal reopening. The problem would be even worse in rural areas of Ethiopia since 85 percent of women live where there are no health centers or medical experts to assist with the procedure. Instead, half a day before the wedding ceremony, women are once again mutilated by the elders without sterilized instruments, which exposes them to severe pain, a higher risk of infection, and often death.

CHAPTER 7
MY HEART'S DESIRE

Kedra waits for her lover in her family's restaurant. Ateib has been anxiously awaiting her reply.

On one hand, she loves him, but on the other hand, she is reserved from any reaction to his quest because of the culture in which she has been raised. However, she doesn't know that Ateib has gone to Jijiga on the early morning to buy commodities. Kedra feels annoyed by his absence; Ateib is often eager to see Kedra in the early morning, and this makes her feel special. As the dark approaches, she begins to miss him and feels she hasn't seen him in a long time.

Maybe he hasn't visited the restaurant today because he feels like I have rejected his love request, Kedra thinks. Even though she hasn't expressed the burning love in her heart, she is very eager to see him again. Kedra thinks she understands what love is and realizes she has fallen in love with Ateib. She believes it is mandatory and natural to start a love affair with a person in the same age group, and she begins to think of him in other ways. After Atum told them about her sexual experience, Kedra felt a new motivation.

Kedra hasn't seen or heard from Ateib in several days and feels like something is missing. On Sunday, after lunch, Kedra looks for him near his residence. It is extremely hot, and she is wearing her headscarf and a long dress. She searches the streets for the boy she has fallen in love with, but he is nowhere to be found.

She goes home, goes to bed, and thinks about Ateib.

Ateib has been thinking about her while he completes his business in Jijiga. He can't call her because he doesn't have her number, and even if he did, her family would never allow them to speak to each other. Ateib's mind is racing with thoughts about Kedra. *Does she have the same feelings of love? What else does she feel?* He completes the deal in Jijiga and returns to Dire Dawa a few days later.

After passing Jijiga and Harar, Ateib arrives in Dengego. He looks at his watch and fidgets. He needs to get back to Dire Dawa to see Kedra again. After the long journey, he takes a shower and hurries to the restaurant to give Kedra a nice bottle of perfume to express his love for her.

Kedra notices him and smiles. Her soul is full of happiness, and she is very pleased to see him, but there is a feeling that is beyond her control.

Ateib wants to greet her with a strong feeling of passion and longing.

Kedra embraces him with two hands.

Ateib says, "What is wrong with you?"

"I don't know what is going on with me." Kedra touches him as if there is no around.

Ateib says, "I have done no witchcraft or magic to you—and now you love me?"

"Yes," Kedra replies.

"I am expressing my deep love to you. Something strange is going on inside me. I was messed up, especially in the past three days. The days are as long as the darkness at night. Is this what is meant by love?"

Kedra's eyes fill with tears. Letting him out of her embrace, she wipes the tears from her eyes.

Ateib is holding her hands and whirling in between happiness and sorrow. The customers and waiters are surprised by what is going on and look at them. They are surprised that such a love affair is expressed in a society where love is not expressed openly, especially in a public place. Ateib and Kedra are surprised too. The customers and waiters understand that Kedra's feelings are related to overcoming the influence of a backward culture, religion, and family.

While they are embracing, Kedra's father soon walks into the restaurant. He is wearing his usual apron, white T-shirt, and cape. His face turns an angry red.

Kedra is very nervous and pulls away from Ateib. She watches her father anxiously and feels a cold fear inside.

Ato Hajji is shocked and dismayed by the situation. He glares at them. He knows what this means. He cannot believe what he is seeing. He never expected his daughter would attempt such a love affair in public and in front of everyone—unless he is dreaming. He knows this is real because of the look on his daughter's face. Eventually, he concludes that it is a deep-rooted relationship.

Ateib is humiliated and ashamed, and he becomes very nervous.

Kedra returns to her register and sits down for a moment to control her emotions. Her body is sweating, and she is in deep thought. Her heartbeat increases dramatically and starts pounding.

The customers and waiters are looking at Ato Hajji. He is humiliated and disrespected and stares at Ateib. He turns to Kedra and says, "What are you doing? What is your relationship with this boy?" His voice is filled with bitterness.

Kedra treats her father like a classmate. If her dad hears the truth, he will be mad at her.

"I saw you together last week—and I have seen you embracing with my own eyes again today. What is your relationship with him?"

Kedra is nervous and frightened. She knows her father will be furious, but she is in serious love with Ateib.

"We will talk about this at home! When Abdullahi comes, tell him that I have gone to shop."

Kedra looks at her dad in complete silence as he is leaving. She feels anxious as she anticipates the punishment awaiting her at home. *Allah is great! You know everything. Everything happens for the good or the bad. God, save me from this mess through your wisdom. Amen.* After completing her morning tasks at the restaurant, Kedra goes to school.

Ato Hajji woke up that morning and welcomed the day by praying, but he feels sick after finding his daughter with Ateib. He spends the afternoon chewing qat with Ato Abdullahi.

At school, Kedra is constantly daydreaming. Her body is present, but her mind is absent; she is thinking about what happened this morning and imagines her punishment. What comes to mind is her lover and the love she has for him. Kedra does not tell Soraya or Atum. After school, she reads a book in her bedroom and thinks about a response to her parents. There will be no one to set her free from a beating. She knows from experience that she will be punished tonight.

At two o'clock in the morning, Ato Hajji tells his wife what he encountered in the restaurant. "She is becoming rude. She starts an affair with a boy. Last week, I saw him acting suspiciously in the restaurant. I thought he was an ordinary client and carelessly left him. Today, I have seen what humiliation really is—and shame for the both of us. While clients are being served, they are holding hands."

Aida cannot believe what she is hearing. "Are you kidding?"

"Allah is my witness. This girl is about to humiliate us. We have been respected so far. I am afraid that she will be pregnant before marriage—just like the others."

Aida responds, "By the way, where is she now? Bring her to me."

Kedra is paralyzed with fear as she listens to her parents' conversation. She begins to tremble and panic. She feels like she is in the middle of nowhere and begins praying to God.

Her mom enters Kedra's bedroom and says, "What is your dad telling me? Whom were you with yesterday morning at the restaurant? How dare you have such an affair with a boy?" Her mother's eyes are full of tears.

Kedra says, "He is just a school friend. We have no other kind of relationship as you might think." She lies to save her mom from the anger and humiliation.

"A school friend is just a school friend. What does it mean to hold hands with a boy at your place of work? What does it imply? Don't you realize what that means? Are you going to humiliate us?"

Ato Hajji begins to beat Kedra with his belt. He drags her out of bed and beats her again and again.

She gasps in pain. After a while, she collapses on the floor and accepts the beating. She has never been punished like this before, and she is severely crushed.

According to the belief and tradition of the community, a teenage girl is strictly prohibited from enjoying relations with the opposite sex. It is counted as rude and disrespectful to the parents' honor. Any kind of sexual intercourse before marriage is regarded as sin. And she will have humiliated her parents.

In her parents' opinion, Kedra has disrespected her culture, tradition, and most importantly their religion. She has disregarded her religious leaders and failed to obey the words of Allah. Those reasons justify her brutal punishment.

Kedra holds her head in her hands. She is in a great deal of pain.

Her dad says, "Tell me the truth. Who is this boy? Do you know what this means? Do you realize what our relatives and colleagues will say if they see you with a boy? How dare you let us be humiliated? Would you like to see my humiliation? That will never happen while I'm alive!"

Kedra gasps from the pain, but she is afraid to tell the truth. She says he is just a school friend and tries to sit up.

Her dad catches her and pinches and twists her ear. "By sending you to school, we wanted you to learn, but you are spending time with boys. Is it because you are free? Ha!" Kedra's dad is generous and has never beaten her so badly. "So, what is better? What shall we do to her? Is it not with great shame and humiliation that Kedra—in public, in our restaurant—is committing such rude acts?"

Her mom nods and says, "It feels like the world has turned upside down. What shall we do? What devil is born with her? Allah, what wrong have we done to you? Why do you humiliate us like this? Don't you realize what that means?"

Her father says, "She has committed a crime. She has sinned. She is a devil. She is also bringing sin upon us."

Aida says, "None of the other children have disgraced us. Anyways, wait until dawn. It is still dark outside. We shall not be disgraced because of you. It is our fault that we let you go to school. You are chilling with boys rather than learning."

Through all the beatings that night, Kedra doesn't cry or say a word. However, when they let out of her bedroom, she begins crying and sobbing. Thinking about her fate and womanhood, she cries terribly.

Her mom pounds Kedra's back with her feet and orders her to stand up. After her mom leaves the room, Kedra lets go a loud cry.

Ato Hajji says, "Where has such a bad-mannered and devilish girl come from?"

Aida says, "In this generation, children don't abide by their families. They don't respect religion, culture, or family. They are cursed. I will take her for checkup tomorrow—before the worst disgrace comes."

Kedra sits on her bed and smears ointment on her wounded and beaten skin.

Aida wakes up Kedra in the early morning, tells her not to go anywhere, and goes to Amina's home.

Amina says, "What is wrong? Why have you come so early in the morning? What happened to you? Are you okay?"

"Thanks to Allah, we are okay. It is your vulgar sister. She has begun having a relationship with the opposite sex at school and in the restaurant. Let's go now. We must take Kedra for a checkup with Mekia. Today's girls aren't trustworthy. We need to make sure Kedra's genitals are still sewed and circumcised. If she is secretly opened, we will have her genitals resewn."

Amina pretends she doesn't know about Kedra's relationship with Ateib. *What happened to Kedra? I told her to take care of this.*

Amina and her mom enter Kedra's room and look at Kedra's swollen and wounded body. Her bleeding skin is stuck to her dress.

Amina turns to her mother and says, "How dare you beat her like this?"

Aida says, "Just cool down. You have no idea about this. There is no way Kedra will dishonor us."

Amina says, "I am not saying that she should not be punished if she is doing wrong, but punishment is meant for teaching—not for hurting. Maybe give her some advice concerning boys. She is still a kid! It is not fair or right to beat her until her body is wounded."

W/o Aida says, "It is not your business. Shut your mouth! Punishment is meant for punishment."

Ato Hajji listens while his wife and daughter are arguing about Kedra's punishment. He calls Amina and says, "Leave this matter alone. It is none of your business. It is we who have been dishonored and disrespected because of your sister's deeds. You may visit us, but never tell us how to punish our children. In your childhood, you were punished when you made mistakes. As a result, you are engaged in a legal marriage. Kedra is not expected to dishonor us. Kedra is living with us; therefore, she should respect our family, religion, and traditions."

Amina is afraid of her father. She goes to Kedra's room and hugs her. Kedra swallows hard and nods.

Amina says, "What is wrong, Kedra? I warned you not to be seen with him in public."

Kedra whispers, "I cannot!" She burst into tears. "I never thought this would happen. My love for Ateib is beyond my control, and I could not resist after not seeing him for three days. I love him. How can I keep my emotions to myself in the future—with this challenge?"

Amina tries to read the expression on the face of her young sister. "For the time being, forget about that. I will tell you later. You better look after your wounded body now. You will be given tablets in the clinic. First, we must go somewhere else. Finish putting on your clothes." Amina wipes her sister's eyes and kisses her face. "Don't worry! We will go to see Mekia, and you will be checked whether your sewed vagina is opened or not. Mom needs you to be checked. Then we will go to the clinic. You should not worry. Let it be checked. Are you frightened? Have you had it opened?"

Kedra says, "No, it has not been opened."

Amina says, "Really! I don't think you will lie to me."

Kedra says, "Why would I lie to you?"

Amina says, "If this is the case, this process should be easy for you. And you can count this as a success."

Finally, after veiling her wounded body and swollen face, they go to Mekia's home.

W/o Mekia lives in Dire Dawa, and she is a traditional laborer. She gives services for traditional medications. She also works on bonding wounds due to ovulectomy and circumcision. When Kedra, her mother, and Amina arrive, five ladies are waiting to seek help for their screaming children. One of the children was circumcised without a painkiller or anesthesia. Screams, shouts, and crying fill the compound. Some mothers go outside to soothe their screaming children. Children, ranging from a month to six years old, are waiting to be mutilated. W/o Mekia's home is very busy. Every morning, it is full of mothers and screaming children. In general, a healthy child will be taken to Mekia's home and will come out covered in blood with one of its organs mutilated.

W/o Mekia is an expert and has worked for a long time. She has generated a lot of wealth. The residents believe her hands have magic and healing powers.

Mekia tells them to sit and asks, "Why are you here today?"

"It is just to check up my daughter." Aida points at Kedra.

W/o Mekia immediately understands. She knows from experience why mothers bring their teenage girls to her, and she washes her bloody hands.

W/o Mekia tells Kedra to lie on the mattress and checks her genital organ. According to W/o Mekia's investigation, Kedra has not been touched since she was circumcised and sewed when she was five years old. W/o Mekia appreciates Aida's decision to circumcise her daughter at childhood and says, "It saved her from being pregnant before marriage and lots of dishonor at large." W/o Mekia praises Kedra for keeping herself reserved for so long. She also warns Kedra's mother that she should be controlled. "She should focus on her work and education until someone proposes to her."

Later, Amina and Kedra talk about her future.

Amina says, "There are some secrets that we keep from our parents. You know that due to influences on culture, religion, and family, you have to practically do what I am telling you. I know what you are feeling.

Tell Ateib not to show up at your place of work. It is unsafe for you and him—"

"I don't really know what this boy has done to me. I love him very much. I can't spend a day without seeing him. Due to his absence for a couple of days, I was extremely glad to see him again. I cannot control myself when I see him. I embrace him and cry. I cannot refrain from holding his hands. When Dad saw us, I was about to faint. I am afraid that I might encounter serious problems."

Amina says, "I understand those feelings. Your love is a gift from Allah. All the ladies on the entire planet are forced not to use our natural gift by men's laws and interpretations. It is so good that you love him—and he does too—but realize our parents' outlook. You survived today's punishment. Don't forget that there is a girl who spends the entire night in punishment and then is sent to live on the streets. According to our society, culture, and parents, this is a big mistake. So, you have to take care of this matter for the future. From the moment we are born until we get married, our parents worry about their reputations. Once you get married, you will run to satisfy your husband's interest and feelings. Then you have to give birth and raise children. I strongly argue that should not be the case. Therefore, to escape from this misery and hardship, you must keep your love a secret and grow up with great care."

Kedra says, "What you're saying is clear to me."

Amina says, "Spending your lifetime with someone who loves you and whom you love is great, but you need to understand that all who say they love you might not be real. Don't give your heart up so easily."

Kedra takes a deep breath and says, "Thank you for your advice."

They hug each other.

Before returning home, Amina says, "Patience is the source of success and victory. So, be sure to take all the prescribed tablets—and take care!"

CHAPTER 8

SECRET LOVERS

Kedra decides to proceed with her relationship in secret, but they are also forced to stay apart for five more days.

Ateib tries to find Kedra at school, but he cannot find her. The five days feel more like five years. Despite his longing to see Kedra, he has no idea about what happened to her and her medical status. *I wish Kedra was in my tribe—or I was in hers. In this world, there is one perfect match for everyone. For me, Kedra is the only one. Thus, I will pay every sacrifice and will make her mine.* Ateib praised God for allowing him to meet Kedra, and he prayed that their future love would be blessed and successful.

After five days searching for Kedra, he finally finds her. They are so happy to see each other. Ateib carefully examines her body. He knows he is responsible.

Kedra says, "It is not your fault. It is some internal feeling that we cannot control." She tells him everything that happened to her.

Ateib listens to her sorrowfully.

She says, "You know very well the influence of family and culture on girls. Moreover, we have to anticipate it since we will confront different obstacles in life. Therefore, we need to minimize those challenges and live together in harmony."

Ateib says, "I think our ethnic difference is a big problem. Despite this, no matter what hardships I face, I will accept your love."

Kedra's heart fills with happiness, and she takes a long breath. She stares at him. To satisfy her longing, she skips class—and they take a taxi ride to the Bangalo Hotel park to spend quality time together. Kedra feels relaxed because nobody can find her there. They order Coca-Colas and discuss their relationship.

Kedra asks, "Is it from your heart that you love me?"

Ateib says, "Look into my eyes. I have no lies. I am not the kind of boy who lies. I love your sweet conversation, beautiful eyes, and sexy lips. I want to make your body and love only mine. I will do everything for you. I love you from the bottom of my heart."

Kedra says, "It is too early to say that I love you. 'I like you' is quite enough. Love cannot be there within this short time."

"Your opinion may be true, but for me, it is more than liking you. You are everything for me. That is why I said I love you."

Kedra says, "Do you want a circumcised and sewed girl?" She struggles to hide her emotions and the fact that she is circumcised and sewed.

Ateib explains, "Your circumcision can't influence my love for you. For me, you are my love. As you know, in our culture, before a wedding ceremony, it is checked to determine if a bride is circumcised and sewed or not. For us, this should not be big deal. For example, it is not only hair and nails that can be cut when it grows excessively. Other parts of the body are made to be cut; this includes female genital organs."

After listening to Ateib's idea, Kedra is pretty happy. She loves him even more. She feels extreme pleasure for someone who loves her—even though she's from a backward culture where an uncircumcised and unsewed girl would be recognized as vulgar and no one would desire her hand in marriage—and manages to maintain a good attitude.

Sipping her coke, Kedra tells Ateib that she is a victim of this backward culture and was circumcised and sewed. As a result, she is frequently sick.

Ateib is sad for her pain and her being a victim of this backward culture, but he is not surprised and takes it easily. Perhaps, it is expected. He would have been more surprised if she had not been circumcised.

Kedra requests that he no longer tells her that he loves her.

Holding her hands on the table and staring at her eyes, he says, "I love you from the bottom of my heart. I have no more words than that. Once again, I truly love you, Kedra."

The laugh, and he squeezes her hands.

"I'll tell you the truth. I spend the entire day thinking about you. Only Allah and I know to what extent I love you. You've got to know it through the things I tell you, the things I do for you, and the way I will be here for you."

Kedra touches her lips and looks at him.

To break the silence, Ateib asks, "What do you feel?"

Kedra says, "If everything you are telling me is real, I will be happy for our relationship and the fact that you told me that you love me. Besides, what makes me worry is my family. I have never loved or been loved. You are my first. We have to make sure my family doesn't learn about our relationship. Since we are dependent on our families, I have to pretend I accept their idea. We have to keep our love affair a secret."

He appreciates that she has decided to tackle her family and cultural influences by showing complete dedication and commitment to being his lover. They are glad they spent the whole afternoon together and share deep feeling and passion. She still remembers the beatings from last week.

Atum and Soraya are concerned that their friend has been missing from school for six days. They know the commitment Kedra has for her education, and missing six days of school is unusual. They decide to visit her at home.

Atum says, "Why have you been absent from school?"

Soraya says, "We thought you were sick, as usual, but expected you to come to school today. When you didn't, we guessed you were in trouble and came to see you."

Kedra closes the bedroom door, sits on her bed, and tells them everything that happened that week.

Soraya and Atum look at each other in surprise.

Soraya says, "Why didn't you resolve this matter? Don't you know this kind of relationship with a boy before marriage is shameful in our society? You know the attitude and outlook of your parents. This is a great loss and disgrace for them."

Atum says, "It is Almighty God who saved you in his wisdom. Never dare to make such a mistake again. Imagine if you had opened your vagina in secret just like Soraya and I did. You would have encountered more serious problems—or even displacement from your home."

Kedra says, "The relationship is the result of my infatuation with Ateib."

Atum says, "Who is Ateib? Who makes you crazy to the extent that you lose control?"

Kedra tells her friends everything about Ateib in detail. "I even missed class today because I was staying with him at Bangalo Hotel. He is so good. I have never fallen in love or been loved by someone before. I don't know exactly what love means, but I can tell that he has fallen for me. It has been three months since we've met."

Her friends laugh.

Atum says, "What about you? Do you love him?"

"In fact, I do love him. He is my first test of having a normal boy-girl relationship. Only Allah knows the future. First, he tells me his feelings. I knew then that I loved him. Ateib is smart, hardworking, and clever. I was able to learn his personality in a very short period. I am happy. I love him. He is the boy I've always dreamed about. He brings me perfumes. The first day we met, he gave me a perfume that is my favorite. It sounds like he understands my feelings. So, I guess he is my type. He takes every part of life seriously and politely. Ateib is my boyfriend—and he is my true love and my sweetheart."

"It is nice of you to love Ateib. You should not trace deep love with your first exposure with boys. You have to spend much more time to examine and look deep into him. For this, you need more time. Mind you, it can be quite easy to love someone, but it's pretty hard to maintain a smooth relationship for a long time."

"You are right. I understand that. It might look pure and true when you're infatuated with someone. As you would start a million-mile journey with the first step, love can also start at any juncture. If a relationship full of challenges begins at some point in life, one should go to the end. We shouldn't be reserved for fear of family, cultural, or religious influences because it is inevitable in the future. Thus, I love this boy. When I am with him, I can't express in words the feeling and satisfaction I have. It is not only his appreciation and gifts; even his silence fills my heart with happiness."

Soraya says, "Let your love extend in peace. It seems like you have fallen seriously in love. We wish you all the best."

The first semester exam is approaching, and the students are busy at school and studying hard. They study in class, in the library, in study groups, and individually to get ready for the examination. Kedra's classmates are studying in a group and solving problems in class. Kedra and Soraya give a tutorial for the whole class. Since Kedra has basic knowledge in English and science, she has no problem tutoring the class. She has impressive skills.

Atum suggests going to Harar for a day after they finish their exams during the fifteen-day break.

Kedra and Sofia agree to the idea, but they are not sure they will be permitted to go. They agree to try to get permission anyway.

Atum tells them that she will use the opportunity to get to know Hassen even more.

Kedra would love to leave Dire Dawa and have fun with her friends. Her family has no way of knowing about her trip with Ateib. She trusts her best friends to keep it a secret. She is confident about spending a day during the school break with her friends. She is excited about the trip. They pray to Allah about the trip, hoping permission is granted.

Kedra's love for Ateib is drastically increasing each day. She thinks about him from the moment she wakes up in the morning. She thinks about him wherever she goes, at her job, at school, while studying, and on her bed. Her friends' advice to love Ateib gives her some courage and confidence about their relationship, but she is having difficulty following their advice due to family and cultural influences. Since her dad is popular in the city, she can't move freely in town. She spends a lot of time with a veil that covers her face.

Ateib can only see her face when they meet in secret. Even then, they stay together for a short time because people might see them in town and recognize her. Kedra invites Ateib on the trip to Harar with her friends, and he accepts. He is pretty excited to go with her. Kedra is quite happy with his response, but it is what she expected.

They complete their exams and prepare to go to Harar for their vacation. Unfortunately, Soraya is unable to go with her friends because her family will not allow her.

Kedra wears her burka on the trip to Harar. They are not pleased with Soraya's absence. From the minibus, the roadside eucalyptus tree and arid plants seem to be running back. They reach Harar, and Kedra takes off her burka, leaving the headscarf that covers her hair.

They go into the hotel to pray together. Ateib holds her right shoulder in his left hand. His right hand holds the Holy Koran behind his back. "Look into my eyes, and I will look into your eyes."

Kedra stares into his eyes.

"Honey, the last time you asked me whether I loved you, I told you all my feelings. I need you to tell me your real feelings without hesitation."

Kedra nods.

Ateib says, "I need you to tell me in your words."

"Yes, I love you with my whole heart—just the way you love me. However, it is only when I am yours, and you are only mine, that we can value and respect our love. As you know, in our religion, a man can have more than one wife. What is your stand on this matter?"

Ateib says, "You are so beautiful. You are a kind of gift from the Almighty that is given to me. So, I love you from the bottom of my heart and with my whole life. Thus, I only agree with the idea of having one wife. I believe it would not be a sin if I choose not to live with several wives. As far as this matter is concerned, I want you to trust me."

Kedra is filled with an extraordinary feeling of happiness. She takes a deep breath, looks at him, and says, "If what you are telling and promising me holds true, I declare that you are also my first and last."

Ateib reveals what he is hiding behind his back: the Holy Koran.

They put their hands on top of the Koran, and Kedra says, "I will never belong to anyone else. I keep my word, and I will be yours forever."

Ateib agrees.

They pray about staying true to the promise for their entire lives, and they agree to go to mosque for additional prayers so that their love will be true and eternal.

They both have promised their love will be true and eternal in the name of Allah. They swear a splendid promise to each other. She will be his, and he will be hers forever with the absence of their parents and relatives.

Kedra, who has no privilege of choosing her partner, has made a promise to the one she loves without her family's will and knowledge.

In the hotel, after returning from prayer, Ateib sees parts of Kedra for the first time. Her hair is often veiled, and her knees are always covered. He looks at her in splendor and praises his Almighty for giving him the most beautiful and decent girl he can wish for. He kisses her plump lips for the first time, and they exchange warm air exhaling from their lips.

For the first time in Kedra's life, she experiences full freedom and privacy. She embraces him, her eyes fill with tears of happiness, and her heart rate increases. Kedra has never known or felt what it is like to be embraced or kissed.

Ateib caresses her long, shiny hair in silence. Kedra and her lover hold each other close on their bed but feel nervous.

Atum laughs and claps her hands. They stand up and celebrate the day, December 1982, as the day they swear to be each other's. They visit the historic city of Harar—Jegol Castle, Ras Mekonnen Palace, the markets, and a popular park—before their journey home.

At home, Kedra tells Amina everything.

Amina stands up, grabs Kedra, and says, "At least God shall bless and protect you from the suffering and humiliations that I have encountered."

Kedra says, "You know how conservative our family is. It is tied with backward outlooks and cultural practices. I am unable to express my feelings of love unless I leave Dire Dawa."

Amina says, "I understand your fear and frustration and recall your punishment for being seen in public with Ateib. If you are caught or someone tells our parents you are dating Ateib, you must know that you will endure severe punishment; it won't be a medical checkup and a beating the next time. You have to keep your love affair with Ateib a secret from the public."

Kedra says, "It is amazing that a one-to-one relationship is perceived as shameful, but the Holy Koran itself says to." She promises to act accordingly and introduce her lover over the approaching holiday.

Ateib feels like Kedra is good for love and for business matters. He considers expanding his business in Dire Dawa to engage with Kedra more often. He begins to plan for a fully-fledged wedding ceremony as per the culture and code of conduct. He knows that it will not be an easy undertaking; for some families, ethnic differences are a virtue, but for others, it is vicious matter.

Ateib has provided for his mother, W/o Newad, and his younger sister, Melika. He has not considered marriage before, but his mother is urging him to take a wife and have children because she longs to be called "Grandma."

His mother and sister suggest Ato Omer's daughter Samia since she has the same ethnic and clan background.

Ateib says, "Stop it, Mom! Stop! You're my lovely mother! I shouldn't tell you this today, as I am fond of you, but you better stop searching for a wife for me! If you love me just the way I am, please stop. I can select the girl I will marry. I can't marry anyone I don't love—except for fame and popularity."

"Look, my son! Samia is a decent and humble girl. As you know, her dad, Ato Hajji Omer, is from the same ethnic background, nationality, and religion with us."

His sister says, "What is wrong with you, Ateib? Samia is the most beautiful girl. She has a sound personality, and she attends school with me."

Ateib says, "Even though you know her, I tell you that I know her too. Her father's fame and popularity have nothing to do with me. I am also a respected person. In my opinion, before engaging in an institution of marriage, love is a must. Love is the cornerstone for a successful marriage. As you are searching for a good partner for me, I am looking for decent and beautiful girls too. However, it should only be me who selects a partner to marry and be bound to for the rest of my life."

His mom says, "When I married your dad, there was no love between us. Love eventually came after we got married. Of course, picking your marriage partner is your sole duty. However, you are late in doing so. You have already wasted ample time."

He says, "Don't worry! It is never too late. I am still able to marry and have kids. I want to be stable to be a proper husband and father. I have remained single trying to provide for you and my sister."

His mother says, "That is true! Let Allah bless and give you back everything you have spent for us."

Later that day, Ateib and Kedra are together. Kedra is frightened because Ateib has made repeated requests for sexual intimacy. The is a dilemma because of the strange new feelings Kedra is having. She made a promise in the name of their Creator, but she is interested in enjoying the satisfaction of sex that her friends seem to enjoy.

Ateib hugs Kedra and says, "My darling, I always pray for you. I love you forever, and you are the most beautiful girl on earth to me."

They indulge in a deep silence and hold each other close. They fall asleep intertwined in each other's bodies, and when they wake up, they are full of sweat.

Ateib looks out the window and realizes it has gotten dark. He hurriedly escorts Kedra home. Looking back on his time with Kedra, he feels like she might not be satisfied—at least not like his other girlfriends. After much thought, he concludes that it was her first time. She might grow to like it more in the future. He has great admiration for her courage and initiative when it comes to having sexual intercourse with him. Ateib has heard stories about how many girls lose satisfaction with sexual intercourse due to the complications of circumcision.

Kedra thinks about what happened with her lover. She experienced sexual intercourse for the first time, and though she didn't feel the satisfaction that she has heard about from her peers, she asks herself, *Is this the only satisfaction one feels from sex?*

CHAPTER 9

BOUGHT WITH A PRICE

A to Hajji and his colleague Ato Abdulahi are chewing qat and having tea on the veranda. They see Kedra entering the home, and Ato Abdulahi turns toward Ato Hajji and says, "This girl has grown old enough."

Ato Hajji understands that Ato Abdulahi's figurative speech is meant to propose Kedra for marriage. Ato Hajji says, "Wow, often girls grow faster. She has grown old enough to marry a man."

In their culture, a girl who has begun to menstruate is considered mature enough for marriage. Therefore, Kedra is assumed to be late for marriage. If anyone proposes to her, she has to marry.

Ato Abdulahi has the same race, religion, and tribal affiliation, and he decides to propose for Kedra to be his fourth wife. Ato Abdulahi grew up in Jijiga. He was raised with no brothers or sisters, and his father died young. When he was old enough, he went to Koran school and even though he had no secular education, he inherited a lot of money when his father died. He fled to Dire Dawa and opened an animal drugstore and shopping center that made him even richer. He exports qat to Djibouti and has made a tremendous amount of profit.

Ato Abdulahi is a strict religious fellow and has a firm belief that other Muslim men should believe in the same things and behave the same way. When he turned thirty-five, he went to Mecca and was nominated as Hajji, which gave him esteem and prestige in Muslim society. For the past six years, he has lived in Mecca and has led a harmonious, peaceful, and fulfilling life.

When Ato Abdulahi was young he was lonely and secluded as an only child. He blames his father for not marrying the four wives that the doctrine allows. Ensuring not to repeat his father's mistake, he has a strong belief in marrying as many wives as the doctrine allows and having more descendants. Thus, in his twenty-six years of marriage, he has three wives and eighteen children.

He lives on one of the blocks of Dire Dawa called Legahare. It is Ato Hajji Abdulahi's point of view that his life is the most fulfilling one because he has never encountered any financial problems, he has plenty of children, he has gone to Mecca/Medina, and secured the name of Hajji. So, in his view, his life has been successful in the material world and the spiritual world.

His first wife and the mother of three of his children, his second wife and the mother of six of his children, and his third wife, W/o Maria, are not pleased with their lives. His first wife was not happy when he married the second wife because she only had him for the first few days after the marriage. As time passed, this feeling of jealousy has been reflected in his second and third wives. All three wives are living in different rooms in a single compound in Dire Dawa. The three wives must serve Ato Abdullahi by respecting him, caring for him, cooking, and doing other household tasks. They also work in the shop and raise his children. Since he is the head of the house, the protector who secures the family from external attacks, they should provide the necessary services for their husband. His wives believe that a woman's life of stability is dependent on taking care of his health and well-being.

Every morning, they provide Ato Abdullahi with his favorite: fresh camel milk. Since his wives are unable to share a dish with Ato Abdullahi during lunch and dinner, they wait for him in the kitchen until he has had his fill and then divide and eat the remaining food. Ato Abdullahi, like many other husbands, has a strict control over the actions of his wives. He forces them to cover their bodies from the tops of their heads to the tips of their feet. The thought that their bodies naturally seduce men for sexual desire is Muslim doctrine. Even though Muslim ethics require that a husband share his time and affection with his wives evenly, Ato Abdullahi gives more love and time to his third wife. W/o Alia is jealous because Ato Abdullahi takes W/o Newad and Addis Ababa on trips to Djibouti. He spends a lot of time and gives more attention to W/o Newad from W/o Alia's perspective. Ato Abdullahi is aware of her feelings of envy and has beaten W/o Alia during the night because of it. During all the beatings of W/o Alia, the other wives have not interfered. Ato Abdullahi, knowing this seed of jealousy between his wives, takes W/o Newad to work in the shop with him, leaving W/o Alia as a housewife to raise his children, cook, and serve at home.

W/o Alia feels like she has been given the role of a housemaid rather than a wife, and she is extremely dissatisfied with Ato Abdullahi. She secretly takes injections to prevent pregnancy. If her husband found out, there would be a horrible consequence. She keeps the injections secret and pretends to live in love and peace.

Despite the three wives not having problems with financial security, they know that Ato Abdulahi's treatment will decrease if a new fourth wife appears. W/o Alia wants the fourth wife to come because she doesn't have loving feelings toward him, and she wants to see him treat Newad how she has been being treated. His first wife, W/o Mariam, doesn't care whether the newcomer joins or not. Even though all three wives have their own outlooks toward the new wife, the man has the full authority to decide.

Kedra tells her friends about the secret relationship with Ateib but neglects to say she experienced sexual intercourse with him on the day of Eid al Adha. The Feast of Sacrifice is the most important feast of the Muslim religion; it concludes the pilgrimage to Mecca. Abraham or Ibrahim was willing to obey God by sacrificing his son when a voice from heaven stopped him and allowed him to sacrifice a ram instead. The feast reenacts Ibrahim's obedience by sacrificing a ram. The family eats about a third of the meal and donates the rest to the poor.

Atum looks at her backside and says, "How was it? I presume the holiday was pretty okay for you!"

Kedra says, "Though I am not sure what Ateib felt, I felt shame. Unfortunately, I did not feel what you described as pleasurable during our intimate time together."

"It may be because you do not have adequate experience performing this act. I felt the same way during my first sexual encounter."

Kedra says, "I wondered if that was it?"

Atum says, "It takes a while for me to gain satisfaction. After you keep participating, it gets easier and is less painful. Therefore, it becomes more satisfying." Atum knows that many girls are victims of genital mutilation and circumcision, which creates a problem during sexual intercourse, but she is not interested in telling this to Kedra. In her soul, and from the bottom of her heart, she prays to her creator that this complication will not curse her friend. If it happens to Kedra, she will be robbed of God's natural endowment for sexual enjoyment, sexual satisfaction, and giving birth without sexual satisfaction.

Ato Abdullahi wants to make his dream of marrying Kedra a reality and have as many offspring as possible. He goes to Ato Hajji's home on a Friday afternoon, accompanied by two elders of the village. Ato Siraj and Ato Warseme bring qat to be chewed after lunch.

Ato Hajji and Aida do not expect Ato Abdullahi to come and propose to their daughter. Kedra is on café duty when they arrive.

Ato Siraj says, "We've known each other a long time. You and your family continue to live in stature since your prior residence in Shinile. Our colleague, Ato Abdullahi, as you know, is a respected person, has the same religion, tribal clan, and language as you and your family, and is a successful man. In his religious fellowship, he has been nominated to be a Hajji.

Ato Hajji Hussein and his wife listen attentively.

Ato Siraj says, "Therefore, we are requesting you fulfill his need of making a kinship relation with you by proposing marriage to your daughter Kedra."

Ato Warseme says, "Ato Hajji Abdullahi is the husband of three wives and father of eighteen children. He looks at his three wives and eighteen children with equal eyes, and he loves them all equally. If it is your goodwill to offer your daughter as his fourth wife, it sounds like she will be moving to her second home."

Ato Hajji Hussein thinks over this matter for some time and says, "It gives me pleasure, proposing my daughter for a kinship relationship that is more than a friendship. Since you are of the same religion, tribal clan, and language, my wife and I accept your proposal." He disregards the opinions of his wife and Kedra.

Ato Siraj says, "We are grateful to your positive response toward our proposal. Let Allah bless you!"

Ato Abdullahi is elated to marry Kedra since she is not even twenty years old. "It is great that your daughter grew up with morals and ethics. I promise to treat your daughter as one of my wives and give her the love she deserves." Ato Abdullahi gives ten thousand birr to the father, and they also agree to provide the necessary clothes, shoes, jewels, and gold one week before the wedding, along with a signed contract.

Typically, marriages are considered based on family, race, tribe, and religious background rather than an agreement or contract. As a Somali custom, a fifteen-year-old girl can be married to a sixty-year-old man, and they relay a proverb to make her accept the old man: "Naag nin dhali karan dhaqi kara," which means "Women can live with a man who is similar to her father's age." As a result, in congruent with the code of conduct, a woman should be a wife to her tribal counterpart even if it is against her will.

Ato Hajji says, "Besides my concurrence in religion, tribe, and language with Ato Abdullahi, he is my best friend. Though he is older than Kedra, he can teach her from rich experience."

W/o Aida asks, "When is he going to marry her? Have you asked this? You know that she just completed eleventh grade this year."

Ato Hajji says, "Her school is no problem; she has learned enough by now. Ato Abdullahi will begin to build a new room for Kedra in his compound, which should be ready after the Ramadan fasting. I have received ten thousand Ethiopian birr for the wedding present."

W/o Aida has not decided on her daughter's marriage proposal but is not given a chance to do so. "That is okay! It is fine for the ceremony to be after the Ramadan, which means five months' time."

Without considering Kedra's willingness, her father accepts the marriage proposal to a man twice her age who she doesn't love.

Kedra's mind is consumed by her relationship with Ateib. She is terribly worried by the fact that she did not get satisfaction from sexual intercourse with Ateib. She begins to suspect it is for the same reasons other mutilated and circumcised girls have complained of. Kedra dares not tell this problem to her sister, but after completing her daily duties, she visits Atum.

Atum says, "Did you feel any progress in your sexual intercourse?"

Kedra says, "We have had intercourse more than five, six times, but it is the same. I have no feeling of sexual desire. Ateib is seriously concerned that he doesn't experience the same feeling he feels with other girls during intercourse." Kedra's eyes are full of tears. "I am afraid the problem might be what I heard about from other girls."

Atum gazes at her friend and says, "I have heard that many circumcised and sewed girls encounter such problems, but I don't think yours is that."

Kedra prays to the Almighty as tears stream down her face. She does not want to conclude until it is investigated by medical experts.

Atum says, "Since you have encountered a similar complication as other girls, you need to be checked by a doctor to know the real root of the problem." She begs her not to cry.

Kedra cannot bear to listen and confirm that her problem is man-made due to the circumcision and sewing. After thinking it over, she decides to consult a medical doctor. The next day, after lunch, she checks into a hospital in Dire Dawa.

The doctor is beside himself even though he has seen it a thousand times before. "It is the effect of circumcision and sewing of your genital organ at childhood. The upper part of your vagina and the clitoris were removed; therefore, you will not feel satisfaction during sexual intercourse."

The doctor's comment sends a wave of shock and anxiety throughout her body. She begins to perspire and cannot control her feelings.

The doctor says, "Please sit down."

Atum is in the waiting room, in marked distress, considering the root cause of the dismay. She blames the parents for this misfortune.

Kedra's eyes begins to tear, and a stream of tears floods her cheeks. The questions that have occupied her mind every day and night all week have been answered. Holding her head in her hands, she says, "Am I going to die without experiencing the feelings of sexual intercourse?" Her heart nearly stops beating when she realizes the extent of the damage. "So what is the solution?"

The doctor says, "Once your organs are removed, it is impossible to retrieve them. I recommend seeing a psychologist."

Kedra's body temperature begins to rise, her heart begins to beat harder, her anxiety level increases drastically, her eyes become narrow, and her nose begins to run. She feels a cold grip of fear overcoming her body, and she begins to tremble uncontrollably. She tries to stand up and faints.

Atum tries to pick up Kedra, but her attempt is unsuccessful.

The doctor calls his assistant, and they lift her onto the bed, check her blood pressure, and examine her eyes. He orders medicine to ease the discomfort.

Several hours later, Kedra wakes up and begins to move. She is frightened because she cannot remember what happened. She asks, "Atum, where am I? Why am I here? What happened to me? I am not sick." She tries to stand up again, but Atum convinces her sleep.

Kedra cannot leave the hospital for twenty-four hours, and Atum must notify the family. "Please, Doctor, she has not revealed to her family about opening her genital organ. Kedra did it in secret to enjoy sex with her boyfriend. As you know, in our tradition, sexual intercourse before marriage is seen as a serious crime and a sin. The punishment is severe. She might become an outcast from her family. After she is beaten and tortured by them, everyone on the street will beat her because she disrespected her tribe. Please do not let her parents know."

The doctor promises to keep it a secret. He enters his office and checks her diagnostic history from the beginning to the end. Kedra frequently takes antibiotics to treat kidney infections caused by the circumcision.

Atum tells Kedra's mom that Kedra is in the hospital.

W/o Aida is extremely worried and asks what happened to Kedra.

Atum says, "She asked me to take her to the hospital, and the doctor told her to stay in the hospital at least twenty-four hours."

When they arrive at the hospital, Kedra is asleep. Her mom sits at her side and puts her hand on Kedra's forehead.

The doctor calls Kedra's mom into his office and tells her she has been hospitalized for another kidney infection.

W/o Aida says, "I know that she has been frequently hospitalized due to the same problem."

The doctor says, "I have traced her diagnostic history, which leads to the root cause of the problem being circumcision and genital mutilation during her childhood. To resolve the problem, I recommend her sewed genital organ should be opened."

Her mother doesn't know Kedra's sewed organ is opened secretly and says, "So, it is only you who can heal my daughter by this procedure. If what you suggested is the only way out of the matter, let it happen. However, we have to announce this to her future husband for the sake of preservation of our honor."

Ato Hajji goes to Ato Abdulahi's home to ask for his permission.

Ato Abdulahi is taking Kedra as his fourth wife, not based on love but on the ransom paid to her parents, and asks what happened.

Ato Hajji says, "Since she is circumcised and sewed, she is frequently hospitalized for kidney infections. The doctor urged that unless it is opened, it is a serious risk to her life. I have come to request your willingness to have her sewn genital organ reopened. As you well know, our daughter has remained a virgin until today. However, being sewed has been fatal to her existence."

Ato Abdullahi says, "We have agreed to extend our friendship into a kinship relation. I trust your daughter as I trust you. Though Kedra is your daughter, she is going to be my wife very soon. I agree with your idea. However, no matter how I trust you and your daughter, we can never be sure what will happen. She can be raped. So, what if we make the wedding day two months earlier? I will finish her living room this month."

Ato Hajji says, "Yes, of course, we cannot be sure because this generation is so fragile. The wedding ceremony will be accomplished after the summer season."

They agree that the wedding, which is planned to be four months away, will occur sooner because of the operation.

The next morning, Kedra is sad and anxious. She can't stop thinking that her parents will punish her severely if they know she already had the surgical operation to open her genital organ.

W/o Aida looks at Kedra carefully and says, "The doctor tells me that all your pain is attributed to your genital circumcision and mutilation— so we must allow the doctor to open your sewed organ."

Kedra is relieved that her parents do not know that she had her genital organ opened in secret. However, she does not know the permission to open her organ came from her husband-to-be: Ato Abdullahi.

The doctor and his assistant enter the room and make Kedra's mom and sister leave. "Kedra, your problem is the same as it was yesterday. Today, your parents have put their signature on a release form to open your sewed genital organ, but you have already had the procedure to open it without their approval or knowledge. We will schedule follow-up appointments, and I recommend safeguarding you from psychological complications from what happened to you. You must consult a psychologist. Hopefully you can then be ready to lead your future life in peace and harmony."

Kedra knows the doctor's advice is valuable, but she cannot stop thinking about never having satisfaction during intercourse with Ateib.

The doctor says, "Though the physical damage to your organ is immense and has caused you numerous problems, psychologically, you have to accept what happened to you. I agree it is normal for human beings to enjoy sexual pleasure. However, you have to believe that one can live a peaceful and cheerful life without sex. If you fail to do that, your psychological disorder can become aggravated." He gives Kedra her medical chart and discharges her from the hospital.

Kedra is thankful that her secret is safe, but she still does not know she has been promised to marry Ato Abdullahi.

After Kedra leaves the hospital, she goes to Ateib's house to tell him what had transpired. He is sitting on the veranda with his sister. When she calls out his name, he quickly comes and greets her kindly. Kedra looks at Ateib through her burka and says, "We need to talk."

"My mom is not around. Let's go inside. I will introduce you to my sister. What has happened to you? What led you to my home?"

Kedra bursts into tears, and she begins to tremble.

Ateib is in dismay. He insists that she tell him what has happened to her.

Kedra tells him everything that happened to her in the hospital.

Ateib's tears begin to flow, and his heart feels like it is being broken. He is absorbing Kedra's pain and suffering. He feels an overwhelming feeling of shame for being male. He begins to think about sleeping with her the first time and many times thereafter, and he sees a lack of satisfaction on her end, which brought the feelings of hesitation regarding this matter. Ateib had heard all of the stories about women losing satisfaction due to being circumcised, but he hoped it wouldn't be the case with his lover. He grabs Kedra's hands, turns his face to the wall, and takes a deep breath. The feeling of humility of being a male crosses his mind again. "This is not your fault. You must accept the situation and convince yourself to live in peace. I know this is difficult for you, but there is nothing we can do about it."

Kedra is crying uncontrollably. "My life is abused. It is full of grief and sadness. I have lost the feeling of sexual intercourse."

Ateib says, "I know how difficult it is to lose one's sexual feeling, resulting in anxiety and stress. You can accept this lack of sexual satisfaction as it is nonexistent. I also promise to accept you with all your problems and blessings and keep loving you for my entire life. My love for you increases every day. You are more than sex for me. You have to love yourself by moving forward."

Kedra says, "I have no words to express my heartiest love for you. Your sincere advice and love make me stronger and vanish my anxiety and worry."

Ateib says, "I will pay for whatever kind of scarification. I want to live a harmonious and fulfilling life with you. Whenever and wherever, I promise to prove that I am yours only. I will also make you forget your injured body by loving and caring for you. Trust me! It is real. I tell you! Trust my love—as I trust yours. My baby, I feel that my future love to you is shining and bright. I will be there when you plan and when you dream throughout your life."

Kedra holds her hands and bows on Ateib's knee as he asks her to forget all of her problems and thanks Allah.

Kedra nods. "Before I knew you, I often prayed that Allah would send me a boy who cares, loves, and understands me in every way. Nowadays, I grew up, and this man-made agony has been done to me. Though I cannot experience sexual feeling, I thank Allah for sending me a boy who is perfect. Allah is great. I love you forever."

They embrace.

Kedra says, "For the time being, I forget my injuries through your love and care—but you have to like me forever."

Ateib says, "It is not only like—I love you!" He convinces himself that Kedra cannot do anything else but accept the problem and lead a life portraying their future life together.

He introduces his sister Melika to Kedra. Melika tells Kedra that she knows her sister and family.

Melika and Ateib talk about Kedra after she leaves. Melika is convinced that Kedra—tall, slim, and beautiful—is to be her brother's fiancée, but she has some doubts since Kedra is from a different tribal clan. Their mother feels the same way.

Ateib is full of pity regarding Kedra's injury, and his sister also makes him worry about the clan discrepancy with Kedra. He is terribly upset and cannot control his emotions. He begs his sister to leave him alone with the true but nonsensical words that she interjected.

Melika says, "I am your sister. Of course, I think she is beautiful, but you are the only one who knows her personality. You have to remember that Kedra is from the Hawit clan while we are from the Darood tribe. We are from different clans; it will be hard for you to live in harmony. You both should consider your feelings—and the feelings and reactions of her family. You are not seriously concerned about which clan a person is from, but her family might take it seriously. She is from a well-to-do family, and your dreams are still flourishing. Can you imagine the amount of money you would have to spend to marry her?"

He knows his sister's advice is right, but he cannot live without Kedra. He would rather confront the consequences of the cultural and tribal beliefs. "I know what you are saying. We are going to engage in marriage and live long in love. She loves me as I love her. Our love affair is mutual, and nothing will interrupt that."

"You know very well that it is only with luck that one marries a man of their choice, and although Kedra loves you, what matters is her family's decision. Our backward traditions are taken as the rule of thumb in this society. So, you've got to take care on your love matter with Kedra. So, as your sister, I advise you to stay cool and think over this matter."

"Stop it! It is over! Kedra and I are human beings. What makes a difference is only our gender; otherwise, what makes our circulation run is red blood. What matters is living together and being in real love. Therefore, we have fulfilled the basic prerequisite. Anything else is a man-made principle. We have done no sin that pulls us away from Allah—so our love continues!"

Kedra's mother tells Amina that they have agreed to offer Kedra to Ato Abdullahi.

Amina stands up and shouts that she does not believe what she is hearing. She insists that it is a bad idea. "By the way, what the hell are you doing? How dare you propose this teenage girl to an old man and interrupt her school!"

W/o Aida says, "That is none of your business. Don't you remember that you were married the same way? I married your dad not by my will but my parents' will—and we are living in love and peace so far."

"I am not only talking about love. What about the age discrepancy? You and Dad were not in love when you were engaged. Even I don't dare to say that raising your children and living for this long does not mean that you love each other. You don't have to let your daughter go through your old-fashioned way of life. You are going to offer your daughter to an old man—double her age, with no grain of love—as his fourth wife. It is better if keep your daughter's will and right. Even though she is not lucky enough to marry someone she loves, at least consider the age difference—and allow her to marry someone in her age group. What kind of life or sport of love do you think she will have? You have to think over that matter and amend your decisions. You are committing an unbearable sin to her."

"No, she is about twenty years old. There are so many who marry at fourteen and raise children. A female is old enough to marry after the start of her menstruation, and she can even give birth. How can we reject the marriage proposal? As you know, Ato Abdullahi is a well-respected man in the village, and he is also your father's best friend. He can marry more than four wives if he wishes. To develop a kinship relation, he has requested our daughter for marriage. He is from a similar clan, and we believe that we have offered our daughter to the right person."

Amina's voice is filled with bitterness, and she starts to cry. "Marriage should not develop because of a fear of social criticism. From the very beginning, she has to know closely, in depth, the man she is going to marry for life—not only know but love him. He has to be from the same clan, fit her age, and win her trust and confidence. How dare you give her to a retired old man? He will die when she starts life. Though she is your daughter, she my sister too. Marriage without the basis of love and care does not have respect, understanding, or affection. Finally, it will not be a sound marriage. There are many old ladies in the town if Ato Abdulahi wants to take a fourth wife. Think about it seriously."

W/o Aida says, "This doesn't need to be her will. She has no reason to reject it. After all, what you say is kind of a joke."

Ato Hajji comes around the corner and says, "We offered our daughter to the right man. A woman has to marry what is proposed by her family. She is not entitled to choose. Both you and your mother were not able to choose who you wanted to marry. What is wrong with you? You can come home and visit your family as you choose. My decision will at no cost be amended."

Amina tries to control her voice, but it trembles in fear. "Your decision is not the word of the Almighty. You are not privileged to decide the fate of an innocent child." She runs out of the house. Amina's eyes are swollen and red from crying. She is terribly sorry because she knows about her sister's love for Ateib. She also knows the fate of their love is at the hand of Kedra's parents. Kedra is devoid of sexual feelings—secondary to the mutilation and circumcision in her childhood—resulting in an increased amount of tension and stress.

Ateib continually tries to convince Kedra to forget, but she cannot and is in a state of constant worry. She feels handicapped, restricts her social contacts, and is jealous of the girls who haven't lost satisfaction from genital mutilation. Whether Kedra is at home or at work, she is consumed with the thought of being violated by the mutilation.

CHAPTER 10

SUPERFICIAL VERSUS UNCONDITIONAL LOVE

Due to the angst that has overcome Kedra, her stunning eyes look nonexistent, she has lost weight, and her morale is low. Kedra quit meeting with Atum and Soraya and spends all her time in the restaurant.

Amina come in to see Kedra and tells her to stop by her house immediately after her duties are completed. Kedra has no idea why her sister is angry, and she still doesn't know her parents offered her to an old man who has already paid a ransom without considering her love and willingness. Since the feast of the sacrifice holiday, she has had a problem that worries her. Kedra is ready to go to college and is not willing to marry a man she doesn't even know. If she has to marry, it will only be to her sweetheart, Ateib, for whom she promised in Harar town.

Kedra goes to her sister's house and says, "What happened? You seem worried and upset. Something is troubling you greatly. What is it?"

Amina says, "Yes, indeed. I am angry and upset, and it is about you! Our parents have planned to celebrate a wedding ceremony for you."

Kedra looks at her sister and asks, "What did you say?" Kedra puts her hands over her mouth and begins to swirl her eyes around. "What did you say? Who is going to marry me?" Her heart begins to pound, and her mouth drops open, but she cannot cry. She cannot even talk for a few minutes.

Amina's eyes swell with tears. "First, you better cool down. I am telling you and Ateib to do is something beforehand to resolve the matter."

Kedra cannot believe what she is hearing. She leans forward, tears stream down her cheeks, and her body trembles. "For whom they are proposing me?"

Amina tells Kedra what she knows about Ato Abdullahi.

Tears drip from Kedra's eyes, her body is full of sweat, and her body temperature increases. She is in denial. All she dreamed about in childhood was academics, and now she dreams of marrying Ateib. Unable to move, Kedra takes a deep breath. She is confused, and her legs cannot hold her body weight. She continues crying. "What did I do to them? What is wrong with me? I have spent my entire life full of pain and anguish. That is not enough for them? They are letting me carry on with life in misery. Why is God away from me while this whole crime is being committed against me?"

Amina says, "This is not the question of God. It is solely attributed to our parents. We ladies are victims of a backward culture and dominated by our husbands. We are required to satisfy men's sexual desire and simply serve to give birth and raise children. It is not only you; there are many girls like you. The resolution to get out of this big challenge is not counted as a sin by your Almighty. You have to look for the right solution today. I don't want to see you married to a retired old man either."

Kedra hangs on her sister's neck and says, "Please, Amina, I cannot retrieve my injured body. I will consider the situation as if I had no feeling from the very onset of my creation. To this effect, I am consulting a psychologist, and thanks to my parents, I have another misery to face with marrying an old man. How can I convince them to change their decision? You know that I cannot complain about this issue. My fate is in their hands, but I am not ready to marry anyone but Ateib. My dream from childhood has been to be successful in school and go to college. Now I have the desire to marry Ateib. I used to pray every day to have God make this become real." She begins to sob again.

Amina says, "Sometimes severe pain is a gift from God. You have to be ready to overcome this challenge. You are lucky because you have a sister who cares, empathizes, and sometimes cries with you. I am not lucky enough to continue my schooling or choose the guy I married because of our parents' backward decision. Then giving birth, I feel I have been a loser in life." She begs Kedra to stop crying.

"How dare you tell me not to cry? I do not want to cry. My own family is attempting to abuse my future life deliberately."

"You know that everything happens for good reason. You have to give your fate to God. For me, your misery is mine."

"My family is running only for prestige. They have no respect for my future. Due to backward cultural taboos, they make me handicapped. Ateib is the only boy I love, and he loves me and has accepted my injured body. I will take everything it takes to be with him. Let God make my heart stronger."

Amina says, "You must do what you have got to do this time. Until then, you better pretend as if you know nothing about your marriage proposal with Ato Abdullahi and stay at home."

"My mom is everything to me. Unknowingly, she indulged me in trouble today. Let Allah forgive her. Though Ato Abdullahi is rich, he mistreats his wives—and none of them are happy being a part of his family."

Kedra leaves her sister's house and goes to Ateib's house. Her eyes are puffy and red from crying, and her lips are dry. She begins telling him what she learned from her sister, but she cannot finish the sentences because she keeps crying. She tells him how she is being forced to marry Ato Abdullahi.

Ateib says, "Ato Abdullahi? Your father's friend?" He holds his forehead with his hands and stares up to his Creator. He feels like the sky is going to fall on him.

Kedra is blind with tears, but she nods.

Ateib says, "This cannot happen. When is the wedding?"

Kedra says, "They did not tell me, but my sister tells me it will be in a couple of months. Ateib, listen to me. We can't do anything by simply worrying. I think the challenge on our love affair is man-made and not from Allah. Some people must trust God. We have to be strong to overcome this trouble. I would rather get out of this city than marry an old man. Do follow me?"

He stares into Kedra's eyes and says, "There is no question about this. I can't live without you, and you can't without me. Escaping should be the last resolution. First, I will ask your parents to let me marry you. Of course, they won't allow me since we are from different tribal clans, and they have already accepted Ato Abdullahi's proposal. However, they will know that I love you. Our religious doctrine doesn't allow establishing marriage without love. If they do offer you to Ato Abdullahi, we will escape to Djibouti. Although there are no relatives in Djibouti, we will work any available jobs and establish a new life."

Kedra is quite pleased and says, "I'd rather live in absolute misery with you than marry an old rich man against my will."

Ateib says, "Don't worry. I will make my mediator's treaty at the end of this week, and that is what we will do. Sometimes life is unpredictable."

Kedra says, "So far, I have suffered much by accepting my family's decision regarding my life. From now on, I will be the only one to make decisions about my life. I love you and thank you for your precious advice during my disappointing days."

"My love and respect for you are so great. You have opened your heart and showed me everything it takes to love a girl. I am happy because of you. You make my entire body and soul complete in love. I love you so much. I am proud that you are on my side."

Ateib decides to offer a present of twelve thousand birr, which he earned while he worked through Dire Dawa to Jijiga via Djibouti. He tells his mom, W/o Newad, and she is enthusiastic to prepare the mediators.

W/o Newad asks, "Whose daughter is Kedra?"

"She is the daughter of Ato Hajji Hussein."

W/o Newad says, "Ato Hajji is from the Hawi clan, and we are from the Darood clan. Why don't you choose a girl from your clan?"

Ateib says, "I love Kedra, and she loves me. She is my type. Our clan discrepancy should not be a barrier if we love each other. We share similarities in nationality, language, and religion. I'll let you ask Ato Mohamed Tahir and Ato Hassen Omer to be mediators."

W/o Newad asks, "Why do you want to depart from your family though you love her? Why don't you marry Ato Omer's daughter Samia or others who are from the same clan? Ato Hajji will not give his daughter knowing that we are from a different clan. Why do you make me disrespected, my son?"

His sister says, "I know that you love Kedra, and she loves you, but marriage doesn't necessarily mean love. Itis a bond of relation between race, religion, and clan. You can't be out of this code of conduct. Our tribe is vast and prestigious. Please, why don't you marry a girl from your clan?"

Ateib says, "There is no way that you lose your respect and reputation. If Kedra's family is willing, it is going to happen. If not, it won't." He keeps his plans to escape with her a secret.

"How dare you say we will not be insulted or disgraced? That you know better! Why are you being so selfish?"

Melika says, "Samia will fit you. She is so cute and your type as well. She is also from a strong and faithful Muslim family. Everyone knows this in our society."

It is not only Melika who appraises Samia's splendor; everyone notices her perfect and awesome complexion. She is perfect and elegant, and everyone is amazed by her. She is always neat, dressed well, and looking decent. Her posture in a long dress makes her so appealing. Her eyebrows make her astonishing, and her eyes are fascinating. Her straight nose, sexy lips, and milky teeth put her among the most beautiful girls in town. Her personality and natural endowments make her perfect. She is beautiful inside and outside.

"I know that Samia is gorgeous and religious. Even though we are from a different clan, I love Kedra. I have loved Kedra since I have known her—and she loves me as well. I don't love Samia, and she doesn't love me. Kedra is beautiful to me. In addition, I am comfortable with her."

His mom insists on having grandsons and knows Kedra's father will not accept Ateib's proposal to marry Kedra. If Ateib was from the same tribal clan as Kedra, Ateib's willingness would have been enough to accept the marriage proposal. "In accordance with the principles of the clan, a girl has to marry a boy from a similar clan. If she fails to do that, she is considered a disgrace. Even if a man marries from another clan, he is not welcome by that clan. Both will be regarded as losers by others in the clan. Finally, they will be devoid of social values, collaboration, and support from the clan and forced to leave. Every tribe has serious and genuine cooperation. They work together to solve any social problems. If one clan member loses his wealth or livestock due to drought or other causes, they will contribute to rehabilitate him. If his house is destroyed, they will rebuild it together. They will make him secure against attacks from other tribes. They will resolve any problems in peace if there are misunderstandings or conflicts within the tribe. Within the city, people from the same clan consider themselves members of a family and help each other. In general, tribal relationships are a close and trustworthy power in times of sadness and happiness. As a result, parents would be cast out of the community if they didn't enforce and make their children follow this tribal code of conduct. My son, please listen to my words! It is not easy to develop marriage with a different tribe. Please don't miscalculate the code of conduct of our tribal regulations. If you marry this girl, we will be isolated from our family—and from the whole tribe.

This is not easy. So, knowing all this, I don't have the courage to ask him to offer his daughter to my son."

Ateib thinks about how much he wants to marry Kedra, but it would result in them both staying away from their families and tribes. He considers breaking it off with Kedra, marrying Samia, and living in peace. He realizes he will never be happy with Samia, and he asks Ato Hansen Omer and Mohamed Tahir to act the as mediators of the marriage proposal.

On a Friday after salat, Ateib puts on a white cape, an apron, and a white shirt skin. He carries his spear, which is the symbol of heroism, as he is accompanied by both mediators to Ato Hajji's home.

Ato Hajji invites the guests to sit down.

Ato Mohamed Tahir, the oldest of them, introduces Ateib.

"Ato Hajji Hussein, you are a respected person in the society. Your entire family, especially your daughter Kedra, has a nice personality. She is one who respects her religion and tribe. We are similar in race, religion, and language. Thus, I have come to request your daughter in marriage and develop a kinship relation with your family."

Ato Hansen Omer says, "Ateib's father, may his soul rest in peace, while he was alive, he was a good and decent Muslim. Ateib is a hardworking young man who respects his religion and his clan. If you offer your daughter, he will take care of her in love."

Ato Hajji says, "We feel proud being asked to offer our daughter for marriage. We thank you for this. But very recently, a member of our clan requested our daughter in marriage, and we already accepted."

Ateib's mediators say, "Is it due to clan discrepancy? Or is it really because they have already accepted another proposal?"

Ateib says, "I love your daughter with my heart. No one else on earth can give her the love that she can get from me. Love is the basis for a successful marriage. I have brought all the presents it takes. Please give me your daughter."

Kedra's father says, "We feel sorry for you quest."

Ateib fights to let his face show the opposite of what he feels.

The mediators say, "If this is your final answer, thank you for respecting us."

The three leave and return home.

Ato Hajji discusses the matter with his wife. He can easily trace how long Ateib's relation with Kedra has been. He never saw him again after beating Kedra. Ato Hajji thought they already broke off the relationship, but his calculation is wrong since Ateib has come to request Kedra for marriage.

W/o Aida knows that Kedra's genital organ is open. "We have to control this girl until the wedding day. This generation of children is out of family control. I thought they had already broken off the relationship, but it seems they have continued. He is not our clan member. We better keep her at home until the wedding day since she might get pregnant."

W/o Aida knows that her circumcision has been reversed and is afraid that Kedra might get pregnant. Having sex before marriage is forbidden in their culture and religion. They decide to check if Kedra is pregnant.

Kedra knows what would happen if she got pregnant before marriage, and she fears the beating and social isolation from her tribe. The result in the hospital proves that she is not pregnant.

Ateib tells his mother about the proposal for marriage.

W/o Newad says, "I told you from the beginning that Mr. Hajji wouldn't be willing to give his daughter to you. We are from different tribes, but you wouldn't listen to me. You went with your will and insulted your family and. Mr. Mohammed and Mr. Hassen. Do you know a boy who is not successful in marrying a girl from the same tribe? Love doesn't come before marriage; the crucial part of marriage is the will of the parents. Please listen to my motherly advice. Samia is pretty; she is from our tribe. If you marry her, you will live together happy and peacefully."

Ateib removes his sword from his back and says, "I know Samia is beautiful and pretty. I don't want to marry the one I am not in love with. I have fallen in love with the most beautiful girl in this world, and I will marry her." He swallows hard a couple of times.

His mother says, "Love may not come first. I married your father without love. I loved him gradually. We lived together with real love until he passed away. How can you love a girl before you live together? Please listen to me, my son!"

Ateib says, "I am in love with Kedra, but I don't know what will happen in the future. Kedra is mine, and I am hers. Allah gives Kedra to me, and I will do everything to marry her."

"You shouldn't have asked her if you knew she was going to marry another person. You don't know your mistake. Please, this is enough! Don't do it again. This is not good for you or our family. Our community will insult us because of your mistakes; it is not easy to live peacefully if we are cast out of our tribe. You are opening the door for your family to be outcasts and undermined by our esteemed tribe. Please stop your devilish doing! As we and Kedra's family know, as a part of our religion and culture, a girl should only marry within her tribe."

Ateib supports his mother's shoulder with his hands. "We spend a lot of time together, and our love is real. I need Kedra in my life. She is precious to me. I will make any sacrifice for her. I will never miss her. We spent eight months together in love. We will also live the rest of our lives together. To make this true, we promised in the Harrar mosque. We did not base this on emotions—but with real and true love. Please, my mother, I know what will happen to you by our tribe if I marry her. Kedra and I will suffer much more from our decision not to marry. So, please be on our side by your praying."

She stares at him and says, "So, what do you think about your future? As you know, if her family doesn't permit it once, they are not going to change their stand. Mr. Hajji and Mr. Abdullahi are from the same tribe. For this reason, Mr. Hajji wants to give Kedra her hand in marriage to Mr. Abdullahi. I think you better marry Samia rather than doing such a devilish thing. You can have a very peaceful life with her."

Ateib says, "I will pray daily to fulfill our future and to make the right decision. Allah will give us strength. I hope."

"Anyway, Allah gives you a reasonable mind," W/o Newad says.

Ateib goes to his bedroom and begins to weep. "Why don't they understand me? Kedra's love is a gift from the Almighty God. If my father hadn't died, what would have been his stand?" He cursed Mr. Abdullahi for involving himself with true love. He considered him egocentric and did not like him. Ateib understands that true love needs sacrificing. His family opposes him marrying Kedra because she is not from his tribe. Kedra's family also wants to marry her to Ato Abdullahi to share him with three wives as per their religion and culture. Ato Hajji also agrees and signs to marry his daughter to Ato. They are all awaiting the wedding day.

Ateib can't stop crying and is extremely frustrated. He prays and decides that he must plan an escape for Kedra and himself from the upcoming marriage to Ato Abdullahi.

CHAPTER 11

KNOCKING ON DEATH'S DOOR

Soraya is not feeling well, and her feet have increased in size. She approaches the mirror and looks at her face. Her face and eyes are also swollen. She stares into the mirror for a long time, "Oh my God, you brought me to this world to suffer! You shouldn't have created me. Why did you create me?"

Allah doesn't respond to her.

Her mother is responsible for the injuries and is looking at her from behind.

Soraya turns to her mother and stares at her.

"What happened to you, my daughter? What happened to your face?" She touches her face.

Soraya weeps and shows her legs to her mother.

"My chance? Oh my God!" She keeps crying.

Her father, Mr. Kamil Adem, looks at his daughter's face and feet and says, "What happened to you, my daughter? You were fine yesterday."

W/o Medina expects it is her kidneys because of the mutilation and circumcision during her younger years. She regrets her decision and blames herself. "If I knew her suffering beforehand, I wouldn't have gone through with the traditional practice of circumcision."

Ato Kamil begs his daughter to stop crying. "It has already happened. We thought it was good for you. Many are circumcised like you—your mother is too. Unfortunately, you are exposed to this suffering, which doesn't always occur. Please forgive us."

They take her to the hospital, and the doctor says, "It is difficult to know clearly about the functioning of her kidneys through a urine examination, but we know there is some kidney malfunction due to her childhood circumcision."

Her father listens carefully and says, "We know the reason for her illness. One of her kidneys is hurt badly. If we remove the kidney, would it help her survive for a long time?"

The doctor says, "Does mutilation go away after her kidney is hurt? No."

Her mother says, "Everything has already happened. You know what should be done further. God is the only one to recover a human's health better than you. We will pray day and night for God to recover our daughter's health. We did what we did unknowingly."

The doctor says, "Soraya needs another examination. She should stay in the hospital. After some other examinations, we will do what we can to help her."

The next day, the sky is at its bluest, and it is almost cloudless. It curves down and joins with the mountains surrounding Dire Dawa. Soraya's body is still swollen from all the fluids.

The nurses read her examination and tell her mother to take her to the Black Lion Hospital in Addis Ababa. When Soraya hears this, she feels like she is on the verge of death. She feels like her plan for life has vanished in thin air. Her tears drip down her neck and ears.

Her mother begins to think about how they lead their life by selling fruit and don't have any real source of income. They need a lot of money for Soraya, and she hates that they live in poverty. Soraya's mother says, "Please, can't her health problems be treated here? We are a very poor family. We don't have enough money to take her to Addis Ababa. I sell fruit, and Soraya helps me by selling coffee and tea before she became sick. My husband is retired from the Ethio-Djibouti railway company and earns only 119 birr. Please help my daughter here!"

The doctor says, "Begging us has no value. We are obligated to do everything we can do here in the hospital to treat everybody, but it depends upon availability. As we told you before, your daughter's disease is beyond our level. She should be treated by a specialist with modern equipment. We do not have a kidney specialist or the equipment in our hospital or anywhere in town." The doctor gives the referral papers to Soraya's parents for the Black Lion Hospital, and they have to leave.

When they return home W/o Medina leans on Soraya's bed and starts weeping. "The girl is a victim of mutilation and circumcision. She needs to go to the Black Lion Hospital, but we don't have enough money." She prays for forgiveness, writes a letter to Kebele to get free medication, and collects money from their tribe, relatives, and neighbors.

Kedra and Atum go to Soraya's house and ask what happened.

Soraya's mother is sitting behind her. Her face and eyes are completely different.

Soraya looks unhappy and totally lost. She looks at her friends and says, "Can you see the consequence of my parents' wrong deeds? My plan was to continue my education and alleviate my parents' financial problems. But now everything is in vain. I am looking at a dark future, and I feel like I am on the verge of death."

Kedra can taste the salty sweat from her forehead as she turns away.

Soraya says, "I don't want other girls to see my suffering and challenges. I am one of the girls who has gone through such suffering. I know I am going to die." She is crying uncontrollably.

Kedra embraces Soraya and tries to soothe her. "Though we stand here, we are not living better than those who died. We feel your suffering."

W/o Medina and their relatives feel sad. The girls seem more like sisters than friends. Though they are not from the same womb, they share similar problems due to this backward tradition and culture. They are all victims of harmful traditions. In addition, they are from the same religion and tribe. This combination makes them intimate friends, and their families have known each other for a long time.

Kedra says, "I will always pray for you to be in good health. I hope your health is better soon."

Atum says, "I will pray for your health. I pray that Allah recovers your health soon." She kisses her full of sorrow.

Soraya says, "I know you will pray for me. I don't know how long I will live, but I will try to live long enough by God's will. I am frightened and a little disoriented. I wish you good luck and long lives for you guys if I can't meet you again. I love you, and I will miss you."

Kedra says, "We love you, and we will miss you too."

Atum says, "When did life ever treat us fairly?"

Kedra says, "Life has never been fair to us."

Atum and Kedra worry that they might not see her again. They curse themselves for being female, and they curse their ancestors who introduced these harmful traditions to the world.

Kedra explains her parent's decision for her to marry Mr. Abdullahi as his fourth wife

Atum says, "I don't believe it. Mr. Abdullahi is old. You are too young to be his fourth wife." She shakes her head in disbelief. "Is it true, Kedra? You are messing with me."

"I am telling you the truth. I am not lying. I swear to God. Like other females, they sentenced me to marry, give birth, live without sexual satisfaction, live without love, and live with an old man sharing three wives. This is enough!" She is filled with bitterness.

"I can't hear more of this," Atum says. "I think this is a nightmare. How can your family decide this life for you? How can they marry you to an old man as his fourth wife? These hardships are too much for one person, and it is not fair. It is beyond one mind's capability, I believe that being female is like being a criminal, especially when we are forced to share one husband with four wives. Our families are decision-makers on behalf of our bodies and love. They try to hear for us with our ears, speak with our tongues, see with our eyes, and send us to heaven with their deeds. They did all this because they never had the proper education. I think they thought they were helping us, but this is beyond. It's broader. You mustn't marry that old man. If true love measures beyond its border, it would be better for you to disappear forever. You are better off as a homeless woman than being a wife to that old man. It is better to live with the one you love without food than to live with a rich guy who you don't love. I think it is simple to come into this world, but it is difficult to attain the goal by challenging hardships due to being female. The road to attain objectively is like the road to death. There are no rules and regulations that protect females from boys and harmful traditions. Being born weak in addition to being brought up female is difficult and challenging. Being a wife is not simple, raising children is not simple, and being a grandmother is not simple. Generally, coming into this world and dying are simple. But living with this world is hard. I think these challenges and hardships come to us because we are females. Is being a female a crime? We females don't have rights. We are governed under the constitutions that boys made. Men are surviving with our sacrifice and power. We are forced to feel the males' weakness, suffer with harmful traditions, and sacrifice our lives. They remove our pleasure organs with sharp materials for the sake of males' sex satisfaction. Naturally gifted love and to be loved are considered luxurious for females. I think males want to go to heaven by female suffering. False would look true if it were repeated. We are forced to accept these harmful traditions as good. Finally, we pass away without attaining our own goals."

Kedra says, "What you are saying is definitely true. Unknowingly, they committed a crime against my body during my child stage for the sake of themselves. But now I can identify good from evil. I don't want to share one husband with three wives. This is why I decided to run away. I need to live with Ateib; he loves me without sex satisfaction. I want give birth and raise our children with love. I will give birth as much as he wants."

Atum asks, "Where do you plan to go? This country belongs to males. Constitutions are made by males, police officers are male, judges are male, and religious leaders are males."

"We need to go to Djibouti. We don't know anyone there, but our tribes go to Djibouti, Harar, Jijiga, or Shinile for trade."

"Why don't you leave today?" Atum asks.

Kedra thinks about this and says, "You are right. We don't have visas for Djibouti, and we must get this soon. Ateib went to Jijiga and will return in a week. We decided to leave town after he gets to Dire Dawa."

"Allah will help you escape from this marriage—try to do everything soon," Atum says.

Kedra goes to her sister's house and explains Soraya's health condition and about going to Addis Ababa for medical attention.

Amina says, "What shall we do? Our families' ignorance and illiteracy exposed her to this challenge. We have to say, 'Allah save her.' We can't help her, but we can continue praying for her."

Kedra says, "Soraya has been an intimate friend since we moved to Dire Dawa, and I consider her a sister. Since I've known her, I have never seen her with comfort in her life. During the past six years of knowing her, she hasn't had enough money to feed herself and hasn't had enough money to satisfy her needs. She became a part of the workforce as a child in order to eat. Her immediate worry is how to get money for food for the family, and she spends most of her time selling tea and coffee. Soraya runs for her education without having enough food, recreation, or the ability to enjoy cake or Coca-Cola, which are considered luxurious. She also had a hard time getting medicine and treatments for her illness due to the harmful traditions of our culture. Even today, she had no money to go to Addis. She is only able to go to Addis Ababa for her treatments because some people collected money from her tribe. God help her. Curing her from her illness is only from the power of God."

Amina says, "I can accept your decision about your future life without thinking twice. I sympathize with you. There are no secrets in a small town—so keep this secret to yourself. Your secret is also mine. If they know that I know you are about to escape from your formal husband, I don't want to tell you what will happen to me. We will meet at home on Friday. Ali from Jijiga, Mohamed from Shinile, and our brothers will come to our home. They will tell you formally that you are the wife of Mr. Abdullahi. So, you have to leave town soon. The wedding day might be in the near future."

Kedra says, "I am not surprised by what you are saying. Ateib went to Jijiga. He will come back in a week with identification cards and pass cards for Djibouti. You know, I'm struggling hiding my feelings from my parents. I can't sleep. I am always thinking about this, and I am so worried about leaving my family. Do you think the wedding day will be soon?"

Kedra says, "I don't know. I think it may occur this month, and I understand your worries."

Amina says, "Life, for some people, is like fresh and soft cake; for others, it's like hard stone. These hardships and challenges are beyond your age and mind. You are not even twenty, and you're too young to worry about this stuff. If you try to solve problems one by one, you will get more."

Millions of girls who are Kedra's age are forced into early marriage for economic reasons, and they are forced to give up school due to their families' traditions and the negative attitude toward females.

On Friday, Kedra's relatives gather in their home, and as usual, the weather is stifling. It doesn't look like summer since all the townspeople wear a lot of clothing to protect themselves from the hot weather. Some wear shirts while others wear *Jelebiya* (long-dress like clothing that extends down to the ankles). Females also wear burkas that cover themselves from their hair to their feet. Some women also wear jilbab or headscarves that cover their hair and ears and long dresses or Diria.

Ato Hajji puts on his belt, white shirt, cap (the sign of Islamic religion), and *musbah* with his left hand. He calls Kedra and says, "As you know, you are no longer a baby. After two weeks, you will start a new life with Ato Abdullahi. We are proud of you because you kept your family's name and respect. In addition to being the wife of Ato Abdullahi, we'll become relatives with Ato Abdullahi through this marriage. Ato Abdullahi is a good man who protects his wives. If you respect and protect him, you will get his love forever—and we will also keep our relationship. You are beautiful and innocent; therefore, he will love you as an equal to his other wives."

Kedra feels tears gathering, and it takes all of her strength not to cry. She listens attentively as her father conveys his decision. She looks down and murmurs, "Of course, he will love me as much because I am the youngest and newest wife, but when I am as old as they are now, he will ignore me just as much as he ignores them now." Kedra thinks, *My family sentenced me to marry an old man and live my life in the kitchen. They think I've learned enough in school. I must continue my education and marry the one who loves me. To make this happen, I have to take my chance. My courage, love, and heart will help me. I must continue praying to God. I have to escape from this wedding ceremony.*

Her father says, "We hope you respect and obey your husband as you did your father. Respect and obey Mr. Abdullah's three wives as you did your mother. If Allah helps us, we will see and kiss our grandson after a year."

Her mother says, "A Muslim female should be obedient to her husband. She shouldn't ask unnecessary questions, and then she will live freely without any problems. Ato Abdullahi will consider and look after you as his other wives because this is the will of his religion. His wives consider you the new member of the family: daughter and fourth wife. Entering Ato Abdullahi's house as his wife is like entering one of the rooms of your family's house. You have to consider and respect the children from the other three wives as your children, but they should also consider you as their mother and respect you in return."

Her father says, "Ato Abdullahi speaks the same language and is from the same tribe and religion as you. His wives are also from the same tribe, language, and religion. He is well-to-do, respected, and a good husband for you. He wishes to be an actual relative to us; that's why he asked for our daughter in marriage. We decided to grant his wish."

All her brothers and close relatives turn toward Kedra and laugh.

Mohammed says, "We are really delighted to see and hear such good news today. We are also glad and should thank our God. Congratulations, Kedra."

She feels tears in her eyes, and again, it takes all of her strength not to cry. She knows she has no right to choose to marry who she likes and can never complain about their choice. She begins to daydream about how to escape to Djibouti when Ateib returns.

Kedra's father tells her to stop working at the restaurant and tells her not to go to outside because she is a bride-to-be.

Kedra is worried about her father's warning not to go to outside and stay at home. It is two weeks until the wedding day, and Ateib has yet to return from Jijiga. She must get an identification card to get a visa from the Djibouti embassy. While Kedra is thinking about all these things, she gets headache and remains silent.

CHAPTER 12

TO WED OR NOT TO WED

After formally announcing that Kedra will become the fourth wife of Ato Abdullahi and not Ateib, they celebrate during a lunch with lots of food and soft drinks. They have their favorite food—rice with meat—and different vegetables, meat, and cooked rice (Isku-dheh-karis) different cultural breads, "sambusa" (meat and vegetables) and traditional cakes such us halawa and melewa, which are very sweet. It is usual to eat individually in their culture, but in this kind of ceremony, females are in one group, and males are in another group. As per their tribe and religion rules, they eat with their hands. They believe Mohammed blesses foods with his hand and not with a spoon.

Kedra starts her lunch with the other females even though she knows what she is planning to do. After lunch, males wearing their T-shirts start chewing qat and smoking *itan* in the fire. Ato Hajji's second wife W/o Kaltum brings the needed materials and goods for this qat-chewing ceremony. First, cold Coca-Cola And ice water are stored in a cold box. Next, she brings hot drinks like tea and coffee. Finally, she brings tea with milk. They believe that these drinks minimize the power of qat.

After this ceremony, Kedra will not be able to meet with her boyfriend because of the shortage of time, and she can't even get an identification card or a pass card to escape. Kedra's mother has been keeping her busy at home with chores. Therefore, she hasn't been able to continue planning her escape from Dire Dawa. Ato Abdulahi has no financial problems and has already paid the *tilosh* or dowry to her family. He has also built a house and provided furnishings for Kedra.

Though his three wives know that his fourth wife will come and join them, his third wife has is jealous of Kedra. W/o Newad thinks her husband's love will decrease, and his wealth will be divided into four wives and children when she comes to join them. She is currently the youngest wife to Ato Abdulahi, but when the twenty-year-old girl comes, she will be ignored like his second wife was when Newad came. This very thing happened to his second wife when she was the first, and she feels like she is no longer important. W/o Newad understands his second wife's jealously and realizes she doesn't have the power to change Ato Abdulahi's stand on multiple wives because it is the way of their culture.

Kedra begins to worry and pray incessantly because the wedding day is within a week—and she has not been able to meet with her sister or her boyfriend. Traditional wedding festivities are spread over three nights of dancing and singing, and men and women celebrate separately on some of the nights. According to their culture, her friends, neighbors, and close relatives come and sing wedding songs during the week of the wedding. They anticipate their turn will come soon. This occasion gives her young friends a chance to express their happiness and to look for their partners. The females of the clan beautify themselves by wearing traditional dresses, and the boys choose their partners. Beauty is not mandatory for girls, but it is usually chosen. The major criterion for females is being circumcised and mutilated. In their culture, boys choose their partners because the girls don't have the right to choose.

Kedra feels sympathy when she looks at the girls who are singing. She says, "All these females are circumcised and mutilated. Maybe all these girls will marry the ones they don't love and give birth without sexual satisfaction. Though I am a victim of these harmful traditions, I will marry and live with the one who loves me and whom I love."

The girls pair off and gather in a circle, singing and performing their traditional dance while expressing their feelings of happiness to Kedra.

Mr. Abdulahi provides different clothes, shoes, underwear, gold, and many types of jewelry for the wedding day. Every night, she prays toward Mecca in her bedroom to escape with the help of Allah. When she is finished praying, she opens a letter her sister gave her from Ateib:

My love and my honey, Kedra,

My heart feels proud when I call your lovely name. Today, I don't want to express my love and feelings because you already know my love and my feelings. The devil, who is involved with our true love, makes me cry and hurts my heart.

We cannot meet in this small town. I long for you now and then because I haven't seen you. I haven't been able to hear your voice or see you for two long, harsh weeks.

I know this feeling is also yours. I can understand your stress because I feel your stress. Though I finished our preparations for escape, I know they put you in temporary jail to prepare you to marry an old man in your tribe.

Thanks to Allah who makes us beloved and will help you escape your suffering. We shouldn't complain; we should pray day and night.

I guess God will dispose of our proposition because God loves our true love. But to taste our fruit and pass the challenge, you have to pray.

I need to steal you from your house, but we can't escape during the day. I don't want to appear desperate. I'm sure you feel the same way. You shouldn't forget our promise. We must use any favorable condition to run away.

Allah is great!
Your ever love,
Ateib

With tears flowing down her face, she says, "Atum, do you think there is a God? I can't live without Ateib. I love and care for him with all my heart. I do not know why my suffering in life does not stop."

Atum embraces her and tries to comfort her. "Of course, there is a God. Just be patient and don't cry anymore. Everything that has a beginning must have an end. You must have faith in Allah. I understand your unfortunate situation and feel sorry for you. It is obvious that you can't escape during the day. This implies that you can't meet with Ateib. Your wedding day is in two days. Make ready to escape tomorrow morning. Until then, make yourself appear happy with a good-looking face. You have to wake up before five—before the mosque bell rings— and leave home. Don't lock your door or window. I think tomorrow is the deadline. You have to wear your burka to hide yourself from being recognized."

Kedra takes a deep breath. "All right. I will do it." She decides to leave town and live with Ateib. Even though she loves her family, she can't live without Ateib. Escaping with her first love who loves her without sexual satisfaction over marrying an old man is like a daydream.

CHAPTER 13

THE GREAT ESCAPE

After a nearly sleepless night, Kedra wakes up before five and stares out her window. It is already hot. She listens for sounds that will alert her not to leave. Kedra heard birds singing, and there is no plant movement. Holding her breath—terrified that her mother or father might wake up for morning prayer at any moment or she will be discovered—she carefully collects her bracelets and necklaces from her bag with four hundred birr and puts it all into a smaller bag that she hides in her bra. She wears her burka over her dress to hide from anyone who may recognize her. Afraid to breathe freely, she walks quietly and cautiously to the door and leaves the house without making a sound. Her heart starts beating violently, and she is in a state of panic because it is not in the nature of human beings to have freedom.

At Ateib's house, she knocks on the door, but nobody opens it. She looks to her left, to the right, and then the rear.

After a long time, Melika comes out and says, "What in God's name are you doing here at this time?"

Gasping for breath, Kedra says, "Where is Ateib?"

Melika tells her that Ateib went to the mosque.

Staying at Ateib's house or speaking to his sister are not safe. Wherever she goes, everyone in Dire Dawa will know that she ran away. Kedra is frightened and paranoid that all the travelers in the early morning will try to catch her and take her home. In this small town, she cannot find a place to hide. He heart is still beating violently, she sweats due to her worry and stress, the hot weather, and her clothes, and she is breathing fast.

Melika says, "What happened to you? Why did you come here at this time? It's dark."

"It is okay. I have to go," Kedra says.

Melika realizes that Kedra is trying to escape from her proposed wedding, but she does not dare to ask for more information. It is unusual for her brother to go to the mosque at this time.

Kedra says, "I have to go. I have to go. Please tell Ateib that I came here." She goes to Atum's home.

Atum is delighted by Kedra's decision to run away from her family and marrying an old man, and she tells her to be strong and stay cool.

Kedra asks Atum to go to the mosque to look for Ateib.

Atum cannot find him, and when she went to his house, he wasn't there either.

Kedra's mother and father didn't think Kedra would flee the day before her wedding. They wonder where Kedra is. She is not in her bedroom or the bathroom, and no one knows where she has gone. They look for Kedra in Mr. Hajji's second wife's house. She isn't there either. Mr. Hajji is worried about her, check the locks, and asks his family if anyone heard the door opening this morning. When no one did, he understands that Kedra must have opened the door. They quickly check houses that they suspect she may have gone to. They notify the police station and tell the police that they suspect her boyfriend had something to do with it. W/o Ayda goes to the main gate of Dire Dawa and checks all the buses that morning.

Ato Hajji goes to Ateib's house with a police officer. When Ateib returns home from the mosque, Ateib is told that he is wanted by the police. Ateib feels elated when he hears the news, but he tells the police that he doesn't know anything about Kedra.

Atum goes back to Ateib's house to talk to him about Kedra, and she sees Ato Hajji and the police talking with Ateib. She covers her face with her burka and goes closer to try to hear what they are saying.

Ato Hajji says, "I want my daughter. Tell us where she is! She is to be married soon, and you know this is crime."

Ateib says, "I know nothing. I asked about her marriage, but you wouldn't give me permission, so I left her alone. Although I miss my beloved Kedra, I know nothing about her. I'm sorry I can't help you."

Ato Hajji is not happy with Ateib's reply and is beginning to get a headache. "You will tell us where you hid her. If you don't know about her, then who does? Does anyone know her whereabouts?" Ato Hajji looks up and sees his wife walking toward them.

W/o Ayda asks, "Where is our daughter? No one will know better than you about our daughter." She puts her hand on her waist and says, "Where is our daughter?"

Ateib says, "I heard everything you said, but I know nothing about it. I didn't hide her or swallow her."

W/o Ayda says, "I know you didn't swallow her. Stop kidding and tell us where she is or where she is going."

The policeman says, "Please tell us where she is, where she might be going, or where she is hiding herself. Otherwise you will be a suspect—and you will go to jail."

Villagers gather and follow everything that is being said.

Ateib says, "I do not know where she is."

Ato Hajji says, "Oh my God! What did I do? I am challenged by this devilish girl. I have lost value within my community. It is true that females are devils!" He returns to his house.

Melika is following the interactions between Mr. Hajji, the police, and Ateib.

Finally, the policeman takes Ateib to the police station for further investigation—along with W/o Ayda and Ato Hajji. Atum runs to her house and alerts Kedra that her sudden disappearance has been discovered.

Kedra starts to panic when she hears her family is looking for her and that her boyfriend has been taken by the police. She knows what will happen to her if she is found. Kedra exchanges her burka for her friend's and decides to go as far away from Dire Dawa as possible.

Atum says, "Where are you going to go? If you stay here, they will be find you—and that will not be good for you or me. They will look for you in the homes of all the people who know you."

Kedra takes a few deep breaths. She does not regret what she did, but she is very worried about the consequences. She can't think or speak, her heart is pumping violently, and her soul feels like it is trying to escape. "I don't know, but I have to go now because it is getting late. I have no idea where I am going! I can't go to Djibouti because I don't have a pass card."

Atum says, "I advise you not to go to your relatives' houses or any of your tribe's houses. You know the current news will be distributed soon. By now, many people have heard about your disappearance. You can't go to Harar, Jijiga, or Shinile—it would be like staying here in Dire

Dawa because your brothers are there. In my opinion, it is better to go to Addis Ababa."

Kedra tells Atum that she doesn't know anyone in Addis Ababa.

Atum says, "Never go to a place where there are relatives. Don't forget that you are leaving your husband. Allah is on your side. When you arrive in Addis, you can rent a bedroom in a small hotel—and then maybe you can rent a small house. You can sleep on a mattress for a while, and the food is cheap. When you meet up with Ateib, you two can do whatever you want. You should go to Addis in the morning by bus. Go to Kulubi and spend the night there. Be strong."

Kedra nods and tells Atum that she is worried about Ateib and her family.

Atum says, "You have stop thinking about them—or you will lose your mind. You have to be confident about what you are doing. For the time being, you must worry about you. Your immediate worry must be how to get out of this current station. Don't bother yourself about him. He is a mature man. If the police take him to the police station, he will be released after a couple of days. Your family will forget everything after some time. Do you want to share one husband with four wives for the sake of your parents—or do you want to escape and live with the one who loves you? Wait for me here. I will bring a taxi. You must leave without delay. Don't be afraid. You don't have to give any clues—like constantly looking behind you. If the drivers know the reason for the ride, they will ask you to add money."

Kedra says, "I am afraid. My heart is trying to escape from my chest."

Atum says, "You have passed the worst. There is nothing worse than being punished because of this by marrying and living with an old man. You better stand up and go to the car. Your parents might come here looking for you. If they know that I'm helping you, you know the consequences I will face. Hurry up."

Before she leaves, they pray for God to arrange everything. They stare at each other for a minute, and Kedra bursts into tears.

Atum says, "Please, Kedra, be strong. You must promise me that you will not cry out or let me cry out for you for taking this chance of you living someplace where you don't have family or friends. You have to trust Allah. Allah loves you and will protect you. So, please pray with confidence. I will pray for you and our friend who is being treated in the Black Lion Hospital. I want you to have this," Atum takes her hand and put two hundred birr in her palm.

Kedra is extremely touched by her gift.

The driver honks his horn.

Kedra says, "I have enough money—please take this money. Please take this money. It will help you. You will need it in the future for your long journey. You don't know what you will encounter on your journey. You are going to an unknown destination. Besides this, you are female. Though you don't need it, you better take it. This money is not enough when it compares to our friendship. I know you are not broke. My love for you is greater than anything. Hurry up. The driver is in a hurry."

They leave the house by preparing the jilbab to cover her body.

Kedra's beautiful eyes are brimming with tears as she hugs her tightly. "I will miss you, Atum."

Atum replies, "I will really miss you too. God be with you always— try not to forget me!"

"I will never forget you. I am very grateful for what you have done for me." Kedra hugs Atum, kisses her cheek, and gets in the car.

Atum says, "Don't forget what I have told you."

The car drives off. Kedra is terrified and starts to beg God and fidget with her burka, which covers her face and body. Kedra prays an intense and great prayer—greater than she's ever prayed in her life. "Please make my journey and challenges short. I am going to a city that I don't know—and please make my destination peaceful. Please take me to my fortunate place. Amen."

The car speeds out of Dire Dawa and onto the hilly and curvy road of Dengego. Kedra feels like she is running away from her wedding and toward Ateib. The taxi arrives at Kulbi without stopping. Kedra considers her trials successful, and she feels some pleasure, but her fears are not completely put to rest.

Ato Hajji is worried his daughter will be late to the wedding. He keeps looking at the main gate with his old friend from Shinile. Kedra's operation for escaping is shared across the village within a short period of time, and many family and friends are now aware.

W/o Ayda looks for her child in the police station, her friends' houses, and with all of those who know her, but she can't get any information about her daughter.

When W/o Ayda returns home, she hears that her husband is sick and has gone to the hospital. When she arrives at the hospital, Amina is crying.

"What happened to your father? Where is he?" When Ato Hajji's old friend approaches with sympathy, she automatically assumes that her husband passed away due to his high blood pressure. W/o Ayda starts weeping, and she curses Kedra as the cause of her husband's death and loss of value in their community. "Kedra escaped to avoid marrying the husband we chose for her."

The wedding day is completely changed. Ato Abdullah sits at his friend's house and feels deep sorrow. He warns the audience that he will give anything to the police in return for recovering his teen wife.

Not knowing what has transpired with her father, the following day in Kulbi, Kedra wakes up and prays toward Mecca. She leaves the hotel and starts the long journey to Addis by bus. Though she escaped her wedding day, she is constantly thinking about her family, Ateib, and Atum and Soraya. Though her family will make her live outside her native land and suffer physically, she understands that they did not mean any harm. Kedra sympathizes with her family and prays for their lack of education. She stares out the window and thinks about her future, her family, and Ateib.

The woman named sitting next to her introduces herself as W/o Hamdiya. Per Muslim religion, she has her hair and ears covered with a headscarf, and she wears a long dress and rings on her fingers. She was born and grew up in the old city of Harar. She now lives in Addis Ababa with her husband. She sells itan from Jijiga to Addis in her shop. Her husband, Ato Ismael, also sells curtains from Arab countries to Addis. W/o Hamdiya and Mr. Ismael have two daughters and one son.

Kedra explains everything about her family and Ateib. The story is familiar to W/o Hamdiya, and she sympathizes with Kedra. "I admire your decision. If you don't know anything about Addis, why are you going there? We will arrive at Addis later this evening."

Kedra says, "Until I run out of money, I will rent a small house and work as a servant—if Allah permits." She rubs the tears from her eyes.

W/o Hamdiya says, "Please stop crying, my daughter!"

Kedra shouts, "Oh, Allah!"

W/o Hamdiya says, "Please don't cry. It doesn't help you, and it may harm you. I feel your problem; many Ethiopian girls have taken the same track as you. Be strong! Allah doesn't forget you; you have to pray. Allah has his own reason he brought you here. Don't forget that I am the mother of females. If I don't help you today—after I heard all your problems—I will quarrel with Allah. Until you get what you want, you will stay with me—if you have good manners. My husband and I will help you because we are from the same religion. You can live with us and eat what we have in our home. So, don't worry!"

Kedra feels like it is a miracle. Her prayers have been answered by Allah. Kedra asks, "Is this true what you are telling me?"

"I swear to God. Believe me—for I am an old woman."

Kedra says, "Allah, I know you are behind me. You answered my request—and you positioned me to sit with her. So, I don't want to say anything more than 'You are really great.' I would like to say, 'Thank you for being so kind. You're so generous to take me into your home. I will be forever grateful to you. You are not allowing me to face a hard time in a big city like Addis Ababa. May Allah bless you and your family. I really admire and respect you. I will never forget you.' This is the least I can say."

The bus passes Nazareth and crosses Debrey Zeyit. The journey takes several hours because of the bad roads and long distance. In Kolfe, they go to W/o Hamdiya's house. Kedra has never come across such a cold place before.

CHAPTER 14

A NEW LIFE BEGINS

W/o Hamdiya says, "Please come into the house. Don't worry!" Kedra follows W/o Hamdiya into the house and admires their home. The rooms are as large as a typical Muslim home.

Her husband is watching TV, and W/o Hamdiya introduces them so they can get to know each other.

Though Kedra feels worried about being in a house with strangers, it is a good place to stay until she starts her new life. For the time being, Kedra feels safe and protected from the gamblers and rapists she heard about by living with W/o Hamdiya's family. W/o Hamdiya gives Kedra pajamas, a sweater, and a T-shirt and tells her to take a bath. They eat dinner, and W/o Hamdiya takes Kedra to her daughter's bedroom. The big bed is covered with a colorful blanket. Kedra considers the opportunity to live there as a gift from God. In the beautiful bedroom, she praises God and prays. It seems like a new hope for life. After praying, Kedra rests because she is very tired from the long journey. She sleeps through all the night without realizing where she is.

W/o Hamdiya shares Kedra's story to her husband. Mr. Ismael doesn't always believe what he hears from everyone, but he sympathizes with Kedra. He says, "It is difficult to believe what this teenager says, but she can live with us if she hasn't any bad manners. I don't want to complain about this. We had the capacity to raise three independent children. So, we have the capability to help her."

In Dire Dawa, due to the death of Ato Hajji, Kedra's brothers, sister Amina, W/o Ayda, and second wife W/o Kaltum are in mourning. Today would have been the wedding day of Ato Abdullahi and Kedra.

Mr. Hajji longed for the wedding day of his child, but he passed away with deep sorrow and heartbreak because she ran away.

"Kedra is not his daughter and is cursed. In my age and generation, having a boyfriend who was not part of the tribe was not allowed for girls. In our culture, we get married to the husband who is chosen by our parents. First marriage comes and then love. Making love with boys before marriage is prohibited and considered a shame and infamy. Females marry only within our tribes. By following our cultural traditions, we survive. Nothing has happened to us, and we weren't hurt by this culture. We live and teach our children to follow the rules and regulations of this culture. This devilish daughter makes me lose value in our community with scandal. Kedra killed her father due to hypertension and makes us ashamed within our community. She left this place with her boyfriend."

The wives feel great sorrow.

Neighbors and relatives who came from near and far are listening and discussing this issue and commenting about this matter. They chat about Ato Hajji and say he did good things in his life. They wish his children and his wives well. Ato Abdullahi also lost his beloved friend and missed the opportunity to marry Kedra. He considers it a dishonor and curses Ateib.

Ato Abdullahi's third wife is glad because she was praying not to join the fourth wife. One side is happy, and the other is very sad about Kedra's decision.

Kedra starts a new life with W/o Hamdiya, and she accompanies W/o Hamdiya to her shop every day. It is difficult to adapt and live in a new town, but within a week is working as a cashier and helping to keep the shop tidy. Sometimes Kedra thinks about her boyfriend in jail in Dire Dawa, and at other times, she thinks about her family who forced her to flee.

Kedra picks up the phone and calls Amina.

"Where are you, my sister?"

Kedra keeps silent for a moment.

Amina says, "Please tell me. I am your sister, and I agree with your decision. I will never tell anyone. Are you okay?"

Kedra says, "I am living in Addis Ababa with a lovely family. They have really blessed me. I'm feeling a lot of comfort. They are Muslims like us. How is Ateib? How is our family?"

Amina says, "He is still in jail. Something major happened in our family … something I'm sure you didn't expect."

"What happened in our home? What did our father say?"

After a few seconds, Amina says, "I strongly believe you'll forgive me for what I am about to tell you."

"What is it? What happened? What are you talking about?"

"Our father was so disappointed by your actions that his hypertension took over. Due to his blood pressure climbing, he passed away."

"I don't believe … I don't believe it. This is not true." Kedra puts one hand on her ear and holds the phone with the other hand.

Amina says, "Be strong. We all are sympathetic about the situation. We are sad, and you have added to our grief."

Kedra cannot stand or speak properly. She is drenched in sweat.

W/o Hamdiya takes the telephone out of her hand and tells Amina how Kedra is feeling.

W/o Hamdiya embraces Kedra and says, "Please, my daughter, be strong." She rubs the sweat and tears from her face. "Not only your beloved father, but Allah makes us sympathize when anyone passes away. We can do nothing once death happens. Try to forget it."

Kedra wants to die and dirge after hearing the news about her father's death—in addition to Ateib's situation. She shivers and starts weeping as she remembers her father's words, unforgettable times, playing, and hard work. In her childhood years, he spoiled her with clothes and plenty of sweet foods. He spent a lot of time eating with her and treating her well. The tears roll down her cheeks. She understands the ideological differences and that she violated her father's will, but she never developed hatred for him because his actions were due to a lack of education and were unintentional.

W/o Hamdiya wet Kedra's forehead with a handkerchief. "Please, my daughter, don't cry. You can't resurrect your father by crying. Allah loves all his creatures. He takes those who he loves. Allah took your father because he loves him. We will pass on this path; we are all awaiting our upcoming time. Your mother is also your mother, and you are also her daughter; no one disproves of this."

"I should have been dead before my father. Even now, I am living better than those who died and lesser than who are alive."

Amina calls again because she is worried about her sister living in strange city with strangers. "You can't resurrect your beloved father by sympathizing; you have to be strong. Otherwise, you will become emotionally hurt."

Kedra says, "I can't say that I am alive. I feel like a dead person. Although we have different ideologies, my dad died due to my decision.

I can never see him again. I couldn't give him a farewell. My mother also cursed me and said I'm not her daughter. The one who loves me without sexual satisfaction is in jail." Kedra curses herself for being a female, puts down the phone, and starts crying.

Amina is weeping on the other end of the phone and says, "Please don't disappoint Allah. There is a reason you were born a female. I understand what you are saying. I am also depressed. Our mother will forgive you once she forgets; you are from her womb. Please give value to yourself. If you knew your father would die, you wouldn't have fled from this city. I shouldn't have advised you to flee. Allah loves you; the fact that you escaped anything bad happening to you proves this. So, you have to lean on your God. You have to be confident with Allah. Ateib will be released in the near future. Had Abdullahi not been involved in his case, he would have been released already."

Kedra says, "I also believe greatly in Allah, but why so much has happened to me is only the secret of Allah." Kedra feels like she can't find forgiveness because her mother cursed her. Kedra violated the culture that has been transmitted from generation to generation for many years. Making love to someone outside her tribe is considered a scandal and defames the family as well as the community.

She doesn't want to make excuses for violating her family's rules and regulations, but there are no rules that protect her for not marrying Mr. Abdullah. Kedra wipes the tears from her face. "Of course, I am living with a blessed family in a nice house. W/o Hamdiya is sociable, transparent, and lovely, and she is from Harar. Ateib can call me at this telephone number. Please keep me informed about Ateib's situation."

Amina states, "Finally, don't return to Dire Dawa. You are known as a wife of Mr. Abdullah in our family and our community. So, your husband needs you badly. Violating the chosen husband is considered undermining the tribe. The people here want to hurt you. Do not think about returning to Dire Dawa. Your secret is also my secret. Please value yourself."

Kedra says, "I love you, my sister. I am always longing for you."

* * *

The police continue to question Ateib. "Where is Kedra?

He says, "I don't know where she is." Ateib knows traditional marriage is considered a formal tradition and will lead to charges.

However, there is no crime for asking Kedra to marry him—even if she left her former husband. Ateib doesn't know Kedra's whereabouts. Though he is happy about her running away, he regrets not meeting her before she left Dire Dawa.

Ato Abdullah considers himself defamed and has no value in his tribe due to his fourth wife's actions. He gives money to the police to force Ateib to say where she is.

Ateib stays in jail for a week.

The people look for Kedra in Dire Dawa, Harar, and her birthplace, Shinile, but no one can find her. Ateib's mother and sister are disappointed in him. They wonder how he could start a love affair with a girl who was not from his tribe. There are a lot of girls from his tribe in Dire Dawa.

Ateib's mother spends a lot of time focusing on getting him released from jail—without success. She even tries to force Ateib to tell the police Kedra's whereabouts.

He says, "I don't know where she is. If I knew, I still wouldn't tell them. I won't be spoiled if I stay here a long time. One day, I will be released. I will not change my stand."

Ateib doesn't expect to be in jail for a long time. He starts thinking about Kedra and his job, and he is angry that he cannot work or be with his love because he is in jail. Ateib's family brings him food, which is inspected by the police. He feels like he's treated like an animal. He's escorted by the police to the restroom twice a day and forced to sleep in a small cell with more than ten people. This truly angers him. He thought he would be locked up for no more than a week, and he feels there is no hope on the horizon. He begins to pray toward Mecca five times a day.

The constitution says that a suspected criminal should remain in jail for approximately twenty-four hours or three days at most, but Ateib stays for ten days.

Finally, Ateib has his day in court. The judge orders him to be released because the police don't present enough evidence to keep him locked up. After Ateib is released, he cannot move freely in the city. He has to be cautious of Ato Abdullahi and his own tribe who are now against him. Ateib's tribe has turned their backs on him and refuse to protect him from Ato Abdullahi. Ateib's tribe considers him as the cause of the scandal for making love to a girl who did not belong to his tribe. Ateib decides to leave town soon.

He heard the news about Kedra departing safely. He is excited to know that his girlfriend is okay and living with family who shares the same religion. He honors his God, forgets about the police station, and calls Kedra.

Kedra picks up the phone while staring at W/o Hamdiya. She is happy to hear Ateib's voice even though she is still hurting due to her father's death. Kedra imagines Ateib standing in front of her, and she is filled with joy. Kedra imagines Ateib touching her hand and staring into her eyes. She is leaning against his chest, listening to his heartbeat, and breathing deeply. Kedra asks, "When were you released? Are you okay?"

Ateib says, "I'm fine indeed. I was released today. I know it is hard hearing about the death of your father, especially now that you are living in a country you're not familiar with. I think living with a blessed family makes it easier to mourn."

Kedra enjoys hearing Ateib's kind words. She hopes the promise they made in Harar's mosque will come true soon. Kedra says, "Allah freed me from eternal imprisonment and marriage to a man I did not love. Thanks to Allah. Allah put my father's soul in heaven. I am happy today that I can hear your lovely words, Ateib. I think this is the last challenge for our love. Soon we will be living together and tasting our true love."

Ateib says, "I will come to Addis in one week. Distance cannot keep me from coming to you. I cannot stay in Dire Dawa for long. Your former husband might kill me. I am longing for you. I will pray for our true love and health."

"I love you too. I am longing for you too, and I am praying for us also, Ateib."

W/o Hamdiya says, "If you have true love, do not depart from your partner. Allah also loves those who have true love. You will meet soon. I wish good things for you both."

Kedra wants to visit Soraya at Black Lion Hospital with W/o Hamdiya. While getting dressed in her new bedroom, she stands in front of the mirror. Kedra looks at her necklace and bracelet, which were gifts from her beloved father. She remembers her dad and looks at her lovely face. She covers her hair with a headscarf. Only Ateib has seen her hair without it. Kedra thinks, *I inherited my eyes, height, and courage from my father. I inherited my hair, nose, and feminine qualities from my mother. My God, my father has passed away, and I didn't give him a farewell greeting. Please put his soul to rest in heaven. Please make my mom forgive me.* After praying, Kedra continues preparing herself for a visit with Soraya. She washes her face with cold water, combs and braids her hair, and covers her hair with a headscarf.

CHAPTER 15

ONE'S LONG-SUFFERING ENDS

Soraya's kidneys are extremely damaged due to her childhood mutilation and circumcision. Though she gets free treatment in her country, her condition is beyond the scope of local treatment. Since the local doctors can do no more to help Soraya's condition, she receives dialysis abroad in hopes that her kidneys will improve.

W/o Newad and her family regret that Soraya's mutilation and circumcision could result in her death. W/o Newad is desperate about her daughter's health condition and wants to take Soraya back to Dire Dawa. She has spent a lot of money on Soraya's medicine in Addis. She has to tell the doctors soon that she can no longer afford treatment.

Kedra and W/o Hamdiya go to the hospital and ask for Soraya's room number. They go to the eighth floor, and Kedra is shocked by how unorganized the hospital is. Patients come and go. Tons of visitors with food and other stuff come and go. Patients are waiting their turns or are moving from one room to the next. Nurses wear white clothes and move about from one corridor to the next. Some nurses are crying for their relatives. Some are discharging new babies from the hospital. Some nurses are removing deceased bodies. Kedra watches so many different situations in the biggest hospital in the city.

Kedra and W/o Hamdiya get into the lift and go to the eighth floor. It is the first time Kedra has taken a lift from one floor to the next. Kedra is eager to see her friend and hopes to find her alive and well. They arrive on the eighth floor and look for Soraya.

Many females, young and old, are sleeping, acting as wardens, or having breakfast. Kedra scans the room for her friend. "W/o Hamdiya, she is not here. I think they gave us the wrong information or changed Soraya's room."

A faint voice calls out.

W/o Hamdiya looks at Kedra and says, "Is that the girl?"

Kedra looks at her and says, "She is not Soraya."

Soraya who is unrecognizable to Kedra. Soraya raises her hand and says, "Kedra, it is me, Soraya."

Kedra approaches Soraya and stares at her for a long time before she realizes that it is Soraya.

Soraya whispers, "How did you come here?"

Kedra says, "Oh my God. Oh my God." She covers her mouth and kisses her cheek as tears roll down her face. She thinks, *How can I say she is my longtime friend and I came to see her?* Kedra wipes the tears from her face.

Soraya starts weeping and says, "My life is coming to an end. Allah created me, but I feel like less of a human being. I am dying."

Kedra listens to Soraya and weeps.

W/o Hamdiya stands up and says, "Kedra, crying is not good for patients. You have to beg Allah to bless her. Other patients will be worried. You and Soraya shouldn't cry. Don't appear desperate. You have to pray to Allah to help recover Soraya from her illness."

Soraya touches Kedra's hand and says, "I'm really happy to see you. I'm glad I'm seeing you before I meet death."

Kedra says, "Please don't say this. Don't feel desperate. You can't die. I feel your feeling, but be strong." She compares her challenges of departing from her family and the death of her father to Soraya's feelings of being on her way to death.

Soraya's mother enters the room with breakfast and says, "How did you get here, Kedra? How did you know we were here?"

Kedra introduces W/o Hamdiya to W/o Medina. "Allah gives me this mother for my hard days." The name mother is not used only for real mothers. Kedra shares the whole story of how she came to be there.

W/o Medina says, "Your decision was right. Your generation of children know what's right for you. Parents unknowingly make many mistakes with harmful traditions, but I now realize the effect it had on my daughter. In addition to my daughter's injury due to mutilation and circumcision, we've also spent a lot of money. I'm constantly regretting having Soraya circumcised. We didn't get the education that your generation received. We thought these harmful traditions were correct.

We don't want to see our babies hurt. We would rather see them doing well. We don't want to see their problems. Giving birth and raising children is difficult. If God allows you to live a long life, it feels horrible to see your children's challenges in life—more than giving birth to them."

W/o Hamdiya says, "W/o Medina is right. It is difficult giving birth and raising children, but it is worse seeing them in pain, especially when it is caused by our mistakes. This is not only the females' problem; it is also the males' problem. They don't want to marry girls who have not been mutilated and circumcised. Our culture feels it is more important to satisfy the male's sexual sense and couldn't care less about females' sexual pleasure during intercourse."

Kedra remains with Soraya and her mother for three days, but Soraya's health doesn't show any improvement. She is becoming weaker, and she can't breathe properly—even with oxygen. She receives glucose as one of her treatments because she can't take food. Soraya's father, Mr. Kalil Adem, came from Dire Dawa yesterday, and they both are awaiting their daughter's death. Initially, they hoped that Soraya would be able to be well again, but that doesn't seem to be the case anymore. They know they will eventually return home without their daughter.

Kedra feels sad when she thinks about Soraya's situation, but she is also thinking about her father and her boyfriend. She prays for her friend's recovery from her illness. Kedra arranges Soraya's bed in order to protect her from feeling cold and notices that Soraya is not breathing. Kedra pulls off the sheets and blankets to check her chest for movement, but she is not sure if Soraya has passed away.

W/o Medina and W/o Kamil follow Kedra's actions, but they don't know if their daughter is gone. Kedra calls for the doctor to tell him what she observed, and he orders everyone to leave to leave the room, including W/o Medina and Mr. Kamil.

After checking Soraya's pupils and listening for a heartbeat, they cover her body with a sheet.

Kedra cannot speak, and her hands tremble uncontrollably as she sits on the floor in silence. Her heart feels like it is going to explode. She feels a heavier weight on her shoulders than she could ever imagine.

Soraya's mother starts crying, praying, and raising her hands toward Allah. "Please, Allah, I know my mistake. Please forgive me. Please give life to my daughter."

The doctor and nurses open the door and tell the family that Soraya has passed away.

Kedra and W/o Medina scream. W/o Kemil paces back and forth and calls out God's name.

Kedra and W/o Medina pull the sheet back from Soraya and try to wake her up by kneeling on the ground. Her father and mother cry, regretting their deeds. Other patients are disturbed by their outward emotions of losing their daughter, and some of them cry with the family.

The medical professionals order the family to leave again. They cover her with white sheets again and remove the tubing from her hand and nose. They move her to a trolley bed and wheel her to the coffin room.

Soraya's mother says, "I lost my right hand, my daughter!"

Kedra cries until she is exhausted and overwhelmed with sorrow. Her friend never lived in comfort. She never accomplished any of her lifelong interests before passing away. Kedra prays to Allah to give her life, but Allah doesn't do anything for her. He let her family do such horrible things to her body, and now she is gone. Kedra thinks back to when Soraya was well and remembers how Soraya spoke, how they laughed with each other, and all the good times they had together. Kedra prays for Soraya's soul to rest in heaven. Kedra never wanted her friend to die. Soraya tried her best to fight her death, but she lost the battle. Soraya constantly prayed to recover from her illness. She wanted to experience love, help her parents with their struggles, and work on plans for her future.

Soraya's dirge ceremony takes place in Addis Ababa with five men rather than in her birthplace of Dire Dawa.

CHAPTER 16

'TIL DEATH DO US PART

Ateib finally arrives in Addis and starts working in a small shop in Kolfe. Ateib and Kedra divide the shop into two areas. They prepare food in one section, and they sleep in another section. Kedra spends half her days studying and the other half helping Ateib in the shop. Although Kedra lost her body and sexual feelings due to harmful traditions, she tries to forget everything she's been through by giving all of her love to Ateib.

Kedra's face gradually becomes full of joy again. She becomes strong, and her lovely smile begins to shine. The two lovebirds are assured that true love is not merely living together for a long time and being compatible with sex; it is knowing each other, caring for each other, keeping promises to each other, and respecting each other. Kedra calls Ateib "my honey," and he calls her "my sweet." They spend their spare time going to the cinema on occasion, their lives together begin to blossom as they imagined, and they plan to live their lives together in Addis Ababa.

They find much success in their lives. Their small shop is filled with different goods, and Ateib understands everything about the job because he knows wholesalers and retailers from Merkato. Ateib eventually employs a shopkeeper and opens an electronic shop in Merkato. Kedra and Ateib rent a nice house and work in both stores. Kedra manages to keep up with her education as a pharmacy student.

Two years have passed, and Kedra's family—with the exception of Amina—still do not know where she is. Atum never learned of Kedra's whereabouts. Unfortunately, Kedra's mother still claims Kedra is not her daughter. However, Ateib's family knew about Ateib and Kedra's life, left Dire Dawa, and moved to Jijiga.

Even though they both left behind close relatives, Allah sent W/o Hamdiya and Ato Ismael to Addis. Kedra and Ateib attribute their success to W/o Hamdiya and Ato Ismael. W/o Hamdiya and Ato Ismael promise to marry them formally after Kedra graduates. They praise W/o Hamdiya's family for always being successful in their lives and for being good people.

Kedra became pregnant when she begins her second year as a university student. Ateib is overjoyed with the news and embraces her tightly. Kedra being pregnant with Ateib's baby makes her happy; she never thought about becoming pregnant since she cannot feel any sexual pleasure. Ateib is proud and often thinks about how he will be a father in a few months, and they both feel this baby will be the luckiest of all due to their financial success. The baby shouldn't have a need or want for anything. In their culture, it is a tradition for the mothers of pregnant women to help and look after them. This is not the case for Kedra as W/o Ayda still doesn't know her daughter's location or that she's pregnant. Most young women in this situation would flee to Europe or America through Djibouti, Sudan, and Kenya. Fortunately, this is not the case for Kedra because she has the support of W/o Hamdiya, W/o Ismael, and Ateib. Kedra spends her days with prenatal appointments, attending school, studying, working, and performing household chores. Ateib assists Kedra around the house as much as possible.

In 1991, Kedra had to postpone her education due to the Ethiopian civil war, and most university students had to leave for *Bilatie* (military camp). Amina finally learns of Kedra's whereabouts, but she is under the control of her husband and can't visit her lovely pregnant sister because she can't think of a reason to visit Addis Ababa and doesn't want to release Kedra's address. Amina knows nothing good will happen if her husband and the community find out that Amina knows Kedra's location. He would consider her as Kedra's supporter and a violator of the rules and regulations of their community. Amina also fears that she would lose her marriage and her children.

Kedra desperately wants to give birth with her mother present, but she can't go to Dire Dawa. She knows her mother hasn't forgiven her, and she is afraid of what Ato Abdullahi and the community might do to her. Ateib's mother comes to Addis because she is longing to see her grandson. She is looking after the baby and helping Kedra in the absence of her own mother. Ateib's mother finally gives up nagging him to marry Samia once she sees how much he loves Kedra, and she also accepts her son's interest in Kedra even though she is not his formal wife and is not from their tribe. Ateib's mother says human beings can't separate lovers who are joined together by Allah.

Ateib goes to work every day, but he eagerly awaits the days' end so he can return home to Kedra. Kedra thanks Allah for giving her the one she loves and the one who loves her. Their life is full of joy, and they continue to grow deeper and deeper in love with each passing day.

The civil war has affected Ethiopia since 1974. Seventeen years later, the military regime is still fighting and affecting Ethiopia's economy. The ruling party, the military, is fighting with the guerrillas and separatist in different regions of Ethiopia. Though there is government and power to control and perform duties and responsibilities, the guerrilla fighters force the ruling party to leave their power. Rural and urban people are preparing to protect themselves from gamblers since the ruler, Mengistu Hailemariam, fled to Zimbabwe on May 22, 1991. Once he left, the country became unruly and unstable. During this time, criminals and murderers could get away with crimes and have no charges brought against them. Different border cities' residents, university students who went to Bilatie, and ex-soldiers flee to neighboring countries due to fears of violence and killing.

Some soldiers sell their guns for a small price and return home. Gun sales increase because residents are purchasing guns to protect themselves from criminals. It is not unusual to see people shooting or hear gunshots in urban and rural areas. It is common for street children, gamblers, youngsters, and old people to have guns and have no problems shooting anyone if they have to. It is common to see dead bodies in the streets as a result of revenge or stealing. Grocers close in the late evening. It is usual to see and hear of people stealing in large stores, banks, and buses. People often retire to their homes early to protect themselves from murderers and gamblers.

One night, Kedra and W/o Newad are waiting for Ateib to return from work before going out for dinner. Ateib always arrives home before eight o'clock. This particular day, he does not arrive home as usual. Kedra and W/o Newad wonder why Ateib is later than usual since it is not like him to arrive home after eight o'clock. Ateib always made it home at a decent hour when the streets were safe. Now that crime is out of hand, why would Ateib take his time returning home? Kedra calls the shop, but no one answers.

She calls the neighboring shop, the owner says, "He left the shop as usual. What happened to him?"

The hour is becoming later without any sign of Ateib.

W/o Newad asks, "Why doesn't Ateib give us a call to tell us where he is?"

It is too dangerous to go out and look for him, so they sit outside the fence and wait for Ateib's arrival. They hear gunshots in various areas around them. Kedra and W/o Newad continue worrying about Ateib, and they become frightened.

Kedra begins to think she will hear bad news, and she prays to Allah. Afterward, she calls Ateib's shop and the neighboring shop again but doesn't get a response. Kedra is frantic because it is after eleven o'clock, and she begins to cry.

W/o Hamdiya says, "He is known to come home on time."

"I don't think he is okay," Mr. Ismael says.

They drive to Kedra's house.

Kedra is pacing back and forth, crying, and praying. Kedra expresses her concerns to W/o Hamdiya as soon as she enters.

W/o Hamdiya says, "Nothing happened to him. Don't worry. He is a man."

Kedra says, "I am not feeling comfortable; he's never been late until now. If he is okay, he will give us call."

W/o Hamdiya says, "Don't worry. Calm down. Allah is great. Allah protects Ateib like he protects us. Please don't cry."

The four of them drive to Merkato in silence. All the shops around Merkato are closed, including Ateib's shop. They look for Ateib all night, report his disappearance to the police, and go home. Kedra and Ateib's mother cannot sleep and spend the night crying and praying.

In the morning, Kedra, W/o Newad, and W/o Hamdiya search for Ateib. His neighboring shops are open, but his shop is still closed. His workers say, "He left the shop at his usual time, around seven o'clock."

Some people claim a dead body was found around Sarbet and another dead body was found around Merkato.

W/o Newad says, "God, please don't make my son to be among these persons."

Kedra believes Ateib may have been killed or wounded during the night. They ask for information at all the hospitals and police stations.

The nearest hospital, Black Lion, tells them there is no patient by the name of Ateib there.

At the Minilik II Hospital, they ask a nurse about Ateib. "Did he come here? Where is he?"

The nurse refers to her documents and is afraid to tell them the news.

Kedra loses her strength and begins to shiver. She can't control her mind or her stomach.

W/o Hamdiya wants to hear about Ateib from the nurse.

The nurse says, "Ateib was shot in Mexico Square at 8:45. He passed away before he arrived to the hospital."

W/o Hamdiya's face becomes pale, and she says, "Oh, Allah! Oh, God."

Kedra and W/o Newad walk in and say, "Where is Ateib?"

W/o Hamdiya can't hide her disturbed face. She embraces Kedra and says, "Your first love—the one who will give you a baby in two months, the one you left your town for, and who would soon be your formal husband—is dead."

Kedra feels as if she has been kicked by thunder—and the earth is moving around her. She escapes from W/o Hamdiya and says, "What did I do, my God? You betrayed me today." She kneels and starts to kick the ground.

Ateib was the light in Kedra's life, and her life has gone dark today.

W/o Hamdiya wants to protect Kedra and stop her from hurting the baby she is carrying inside her womb.

Kedra forgets about her pregnancy due to her immense grief.

W/o Newad starts crying severely.

Kedra can't control herself. She feels like a bullet has pierced her heart as the nurses tell them to take the dead body from the hospital.

The nurse explains that they found him between two other dead bodies. He is covered by white sheets, and his name is written on them.

Kedra wants to check to see whether it is Ateib or not, and she pulls off the sheets and sees her husband's lifeless body. His body is covered in blood, his eyes are closed, and his mouth is open. Ateib is dead.

Kedra embraces Ateib's bloody body and screams, "Please, my God, take me instead of him. I can't live without him. He is like the bone of my bones, flesh of my flesh, and now only my flesh remains in this world."

W/o Hamdiya calls her husband and tells him everything. He arrives at the hospital and is hurt by what he sees. Kedra's situation is extremely disturbing.

Kedra says, "I lost my love. I am alone. Ateib spent the night on this trolley without comfort."

They all sympathize with her and cry together. They understand her pain and know Kedra has no close relatives in Addis. Those who knew them around Merkato gather in the hospital after they hear about Ateib's death. Some of them express their sorrow by crying; others sympathize with Kedra by thinking about Kedra and the unborn child.

Ato Ismael signs the release documents and takes Ateib's body.

According to their religion's rule, males must accompany the dead body to the dirge place. However, Kedra embraces his body and says, "I don't want to leave my love. I don't want to give him to you. He is my honey. He is my best friend. I am pregnant with his baby. Please don't take him away from me. Ateib can't get comfort without me—and I without him."

Ateib's friends and neighbors are disturbed by what happened to him. They separate Kedra from Ateib's body with great effort.

W/o Hamdiya and other women encourage Kedra not to hurt, but she has lost her first and only love—and she feels like part of her body is buried with him. As Ateib's dead body is taken into the dirge place, Kedra is extremely tired from lack of sleep and all that she's experienced. Her tears have dried up, and her lips and mouth are dry. Kedra wants to know how Ateib died and says, "Who killed him?"

Amina is disturbed when she hears about the situation from W/o Hamdiya. "If our mother doesn't go to Kedra's home after three years, she will no longer be my mother." Amina goes to her mother's house to explain Kedra's situation. She tells her mother everything about Kedra, her pregnancy, and her husband's death.

Her mother replies, "Unmarried women are the property and under control of their parents. Married women are the property of their husbands. She is a widow now and has no protector."

All night, W/o Ayda thinks and dreams about Kedra. She dreams about a young Kedra asking her mother to buy halawa and crying. Her mother doesn't want to know where Kedra has been for the past three years. She still hasn't forgiven Kedra for running away and not marrying the chosen husband rather than choosing to marry the one who is not from her tribe. She is the cause of her father's death, and she also ruined their respected name.

Amina begs her mother to be on Kedra's side during her critical time and threatens that she will be angry with Allah. Her mother agrees to visit Kedra.

W/o Ayda, Mr. Hajji's second wife, W/o Kaltum, Amina, and Mohammed and his child go to Addis on the first bus. They arrived in Addis in the late evening.

Kedra, W/o Hamdiya, W/o Newad, Melika, Atum, and some neighbors sit at her house to and their condolence. The males are outside chewing qat under the tent or playing cards. Though these people are gathered in the house and tent day and night, they cannot resurrect her love, and they cannot stop Kedra from crying all day and night. Kedra's heart feels sorrow, and she feels very unlucky.

The Dire Dawa guests arrive at Kedra's house by taxi, but Kedra isn't expecting them because she knows Amina cannot go without her husband's permission.

Kedra can't believe her eyes when her family is standing in front of her. It is surprising and shocking to her, and it seems like a daydream to see her mother, sister, brother, and W/o Kaltum after three years. Kedra stands and embraces her mother.

W/o Ayda sees her pregnant daughter, and they start crying together. Kedra's mother regrets not seeing her daughter for three years and for cursing her. She sympathizes with Kedra during this critical time and asks Kedra to forgive her for what she did unknowingly. W/o Ayda is following the rules of their culture and acting out of anger. She cursed Kedra due to her husband's death, and she considers herself a criminal. W/o Ayda says, "I think this happened to you because I cursed you."

Kedra forgives her mother, and they place their hands on each other's shoulder and welcome all the guests. Amina and Kedra embrace each other and cry for a long time.

W/o Hamdiya tries to separate them and says, "This is enough."

Amina places her hands on her sister's shoulder and says, "Be strong, my sister. We all feel your pain, and we sympathize with you." She cleans the tears from Kedra's face.

According to their culture, after a husband dies, the woman stays home for five months. Her mother, sister, and W/o Newad stay in Addis to grieve with Kedra, and they are longing to see the child in two months.

Though time has passed, Kedra still can't believe Ateib is gone. She can't believe it's true; she feels like it's a dream. She recalls how he went to the shop one morning as usual—never to return. She often stares at the gate to look for her husband, but Ateib is gone. He will never come back again. Kedra dislikes sleeping in the bed she shared with Ateib because she smells his scent at night and early in the morning. Kedra is having difficulty adapting, but her mother, sister, and W/o Newad live with her to share in her grief.

When she is home alone, Kedra thinks about Ateib. She dreams about him at night, and she sometimes wakes up in the middle of the night sobbing. Kedra is eight months pregnant and needs plenty of rest. Kedra is extremely restless thinking about her future and the death of Ateib.

At thirty-eight weeks, she starts feeling labor pains. Her sister, her mother, and W/o Newad are with her throughout labor; it is hard for Kedra, but she gives birth to a baby boy who looks just like his father. Though Kedra feels happy giving birth peacefully, she cries about Ateib and their newborn baby. Kedra's future of marrying the one she loves will no longer be a reality, but she gives birth to his child, and after a week, the baby takes his father's name.

Kedra says, "I don't want to see what happened to me—due to the influence of our traditions, culture, and tribe—happen to others. Life is not meaningful to me anymore. I only lived four years out of my twenty-three years of life. I was loved for four years. I am proud to have loved a man like Ateib. I will be happy to have my son in my life instead of my love Ateib. One thing is certain; my life will never be the same again." Kedra starts weeping as she reminisces about Ateib's love, their first real kiss, and him supporting her education. She remembers how Ateib kissed her and how he touched her body after she became pregnant.

Kedra's tears will not stop flowing. They slowly pour from her eyes like a bottomless well. Ateib was her first and last man. The only good thing in Kedra's life was the lovely times she spent with Ateib. She'll never forget the love they shared or the triumph imposed upon them due to her culture, traditions and family.

Kedra kisses her son and decides to raise him as a single parent, acting as both mother and father. Kedra decides to teach him about his mother and father's love story and the challenges of his female counterparts. Kedra hopes to raise her son to be an outstanding citizen. Kedra doesn't want to return to Dire Dawa, and she continues working on her education. She finally graduates in pharmacy, and she plans to succeed based on her education.

THE CONCLUSION OF THE MATTER

Kedra's whole life has changed. Today, she is financially stable, but she is a lonely single mother. Kedra's money can't resurrect her happiness or bring her joy. Kedra has drifted into a world of bitter memories. Though Kedra can't move beyond her past, she has learned self-confidence, friendship, respect, love, and the difference between religion and culture. She finally experienced true love without sexual satisfaction.

Kedra's story is one of love, bravery, suffering, patience, hurt, pain, and finding strength through weakness. She is the product of her culture's ignorance. She is birthed into a world in which her body doesn't belong to her. Decisions to mutilate and circumcise her female organs at a young age left no room for her to plea bargain. She is too young to fight her case; therefore, she endured a trauma that changed her life forever.

Thanks for following this story to the end—and remember, ladies, value your treasures.

www.ingramcontent.com/pod-product-compliance
Lightning Source LLC
Chambersburg PA
CBHW031129250726
48655CB00002B/578